# the personal
# brandwagon
(...and how to jump on it)

## Tessa Hood

Changing people's perceptions about you

The Personal Brandwagon (...and how to jump on it)
© Tessa Hood 2006
Changing Gear Limited, UK.

**Illustrations** by Hilary J. Kidd 016974 76502
**Photographs** licensed from copyright owners
**Cover design** by Drawbridge Creative Partners Ltd
**Page design and setting** by Jaquetta Trueman, Graphic Solutions
**Book set** in Gill Sans Light

**First published in 2006 by Ecademy Press**

**Contact:**
Ecademy Press
6, Woodland Rise
Penryn
Cornwall UK
TR10 8QD.

info@ecademy-press.com

**Printed and Bound** by Antony Rowe Ltd, Eastbourne

The right of Tessa Hood to be identified as the author of this work has been asserted in accordance with sections 77 and 78 of the Copyright Designs and Patents Act 1988.

**The Real Game's Personal Values Workbook** by kind permission of Jonathan Stanley, The Real Game (www.therealgame.biz).

All rights reserved. No part of this publication may be reproduced in any material form (including photocopying or storing in any medium by electronicmeans and whether or not transiently or incidentally to some other use of this publication) without the written permission of the copyright holder except in accordance with the provisions of the Copyright, Designs and Patents Act 1988. Applications for the Copyright holders written permission to reproduce any part of this publication should be addressed to the publishers.

This book is dedicated to John,

thank you for all your love, support and encouragement

# About Tessa Hood

Tessa Hood is the Founder and MD of Changing Gear Limited.

She is no stranger to working in environments where personal branding is vitally important in playing a crucial role in optimising performance.

Early in Tessa's career she worked in the diplomatic corps working alongside Ministers, and M.E.P.'s at the Court of Human Rights in Strasbourg.

Tessa then moved to the film and television industry and there developed an unparalleled wealth of knowledge in branding, image and its manipulation.

Tessa demonstrates to the corporate world the vital importance of personal executive 'branding'. By providing the tools an organisation needs to build a great brand through its personnel, she adds the finishing touch to corporate and executive training.

This is done through several modules and can be tailored as a bespoke, 'cherry-picked' package or delivered in single units. The modules consist of Personal Impact (how we physically present ourselves), Core Values (how we are perceived by others), Corporate Manners and Etiquette (dining skills and a 'how-to' of high level entertainment), and Effective Networking (to build a better network and a greater visible presence in the marketplace). These packages are receiving a particularly strong response from HR Managers and recruitment companies.

Her current clients include Cranfield University Business School MBA Programme, The Association of M.B.A.'s, HSBC, Standard Chartered Bank, BUPA International and British Airways, GAM (previously, Global Asset Management), Harrods Urban Retreat and many SME's, and individual executives.

Tessa's company also runs the Changing Gear Academy for Image Consultants holding regular training courses throughout the year for those people wanting to become professional Image Consultants. For further information do contact Tessa Hood through the website.

Tessa is also a Full Member of the Professional Speakers Association and Affiliated to the Federation of Image Consultants.

You can find more about Tessa Hood and her company Changing Gear Limited at www.changinggear.net and click on the 'corporate' button.

## Acknowledgements:

No book is written without help, and I would like to thank some of the people who have shared their knowledge, time and enthusiasm with me to get, this, my first book, on the shelves.

Firstly, to Ken Timbers, who patiently read through every word and edited the first manuscript for me, and helped me to avoid a few embarrassing faux pas in my grammar, spelling and long windedness! Thank you too to John and Sandie Timbers who helped with editing and provided expertise without which I would have been lost.

To Hilary Kidd who did all the fabulous drawings in the book. Hilary listened to me and came up with exactly what I required quickly, amusingly and professionally. She's a great fashion illustrator, and a lovely person.

To Alan Stratford who designed the cover and who has been a tower of design strength and patience over the past year.

I'd like to thank Carol Spencer of Style Directions without whose professional help and thorough and sympathetic training this journey would never have been started, and Lesley Everett who has always been there with advice, recommendations and support when I needed her.

A special word of thanks for Jonathan Stanley who allowed me to use his Personal Values Workbook as an appendix to this book. His business 'The Real Game' helps people to define their personal values and achieve an accurate aspect of who they really are. Do take a look at his website www.therealgame.biz.

Thank you too to Mindy Gibbins-Klein who helped me 'birth' this book through her Book Midwife services! Her persistence and belief kept me on track and focused.

I am part of a small mentoring group and I would like to thank the members of that group who kept my spirits up and enthusiastically applauded every finished chapter; Cindy Gilbert, Cindy-Michelle Waterfield, Ian Plumbley, Graham Yemm and Sue Firth, all of whom have taken time out of their busy schedules to give me one to one advice and support.

Finally, a big thank you to those kind people who allowed their references to be used in and on the cover of my book – I'll forever be in your debt!

Thank you to everyone from the bottom of my heart.

Tessa

# Contents

| | | |
|---|---|---|
| Acknowledgements | | 5 |
| Introduction | | 9 |
| Chapter 1 | What is a Personal Brand? | 13 |
| Chapter 2 | Suit the 21st Century | 25 |
| Chapter 3 | Goals and Visions | 37 |
| Chapter 4 | Women's Issues | 49 |
| Chapter 5 | Men's Issues | 85 |
| Chapter 6 | Colour Matters! | 113 |
| Chapter 7 | Conveying the Message | 129 |
| Chapter 8 | What People Say About Changing Gear | 153 |
| Appendix | Jonathan Stanley's 'The Real Game' Personal Values Books | 161 |

# Introduction

To make career strides and improve your social standing in the 21$^{st}$ Century, you need something that makes you stand out from your competitors and peers—your own Unique Selling Point (USP). We all have our own unique DNA, so why not take that premise and use it to develop your own Personal Brand that is as unique to you as your DNA?

I assume you picked up this book because you are serious about developing your career; that you would like more power and influence in order to reach the targets you are setting for yourself. Have you ever wanted to have a more positive influence over the people who can influence your success? Well, using all the skills and assets that you have at your fingertips you can build a brand for yourself, just like the corporate brands we see every day. But this time it will be a well-defined Personal Brand of your own and an essential part of your future success.

People buy people—they decide, sometimes very quickly, whether they like you, trust you, can do business with you and whether you have similar values to their own. Developing a good Personal Brand will make it clear to them that you can add value to their business and their lives.

George Bernard Shaw wrote:

> *"Life is not about finding yourself, it is about creating yourself."*

Right on George! This is what this book is about, finding your own special Personal Brand, developing it and showing it off to the world—no false modesty, but with total honesty and without cynicism.

It takes just a little knowledge to be able to develop your own brand and that is why I am giving you here something of what the professional brand-makers do for those who feel they need it, or who must have a change or improvement. We will look at the essential elements needed to develop your own Personal Brand from the inside out and then look at the style and other requirements which will become your 'packaging' on the product you—**ID-YOU©**.

## SNAKE OR LADDER?

Everyone has played Snakes and Ladders. You remember how, when everyone else seemed to be up several rungs on the ladder you were sometimes slithering down the snake? But life isn't a game and in the real world it's not the roll of the dice that moves you up or down the career ladder, and it's not just 'chance' either. This book will show you how to load the dice in your favour and enable you to achieve your goals by improving the odds. It will give you a much better chance of winning the game.

The analogy of Snakes and Ladders clarifies the process of getting you up the ladder of success. If you present your Personal Brand in the right way—i.e. knowing and broadcasting your core values, showing a consistency of behaviour that underlines your character and professionalism, together with clever dressing and good grooming—you will get on the ladder going up. If you don't understand what your Personal Brand says about you—i.e. doing it the wrong way by behaving inconsistently, showing poor dress sense, poor grooming and not understanding the importance of first impressions, then you could find yourself on a disastrous sequence of slides down the snakes.

For many years, I have been an international personal branding strategist for individuals and for groups within global banks, financial institutions, insurance companies, airlines and business schools. These organisations and the people within them find they can improve their chances of success through presenting a better brand. Using workshops, seminars and personal, one-to-one consultations, I have helped them to build a successful differentiation, a USP, within the company. This improves their career prospects, helps to define themselves with peers and superiors at work and, of course, enhances life out of the office as well.

## Chapter One

*"The only corner of the universe that you can be certain of improving is yourself."* Aldous Huxley

## What is a Personal Brand?

We all have a Personal Brand, whether we design it consciously or not. Our childhood heavily influences our self-worth and self-image and these experiences can be carried through to adulthood and influence us hugely. We broadcast our Personal Brand on a daily basis through dress, personal grooming, body language, tone of voice, our own core values, our personal beliefs and what we stand for. This shows the world what we want them to think about us, but we sometimes forget that our own perceived view of our 'brand' may not equate with what others think of us.

There are many examples of great branding. As you read this, who doesn't have a picture in their mind of corporate brands such as Coca Cola, McDonalds, Ferrari, Kentucky Fried Chicken, and Harrods amongst thousands of others. Towns and cities become branded – New York is 'The Big Apple' for example – but there are great Personal Brands too. Think of Virgin Airways and Richard Branson comes automatically to mind, despite a reputation for breaking the rules, his extraordinary record attempts in a balloon and on a super-speedboat, and even his cross-dressing in a bridal gown and veil to publicise his bridal business all add to the public perception of his brand, and through him to his business's brand. Madonna's personal brand is as a great entertainer, but she changes her product 'packaging' with each new CD she develops and has become famous for her chameleon-like quality – a huge part of her brand. You can also see how a personal brand can be damaged. Michael Jackson was one of the world's greatest entertainers, but recent bad publicity has lost him status and tainted the integrity of his personal brand.

Winston Churchill had a great brand even in the days when image gurus and media spin doctors had no place in society and there was little understanding of building a personal brand especially in politics. The name Winston Churchill brings with it a picture of a bulldog of a man, indomitable, highly principled, sucking a massive cigar, the epitome of British stoicism. He milked his image: he knew very well that he was the force behind whom we all ranged against the enemy in WWII, and he used his wonderful voice and rousing speeches, his ample frame, his cigar and his Victory V sign to build as formidable an image as he could to present his certainty that what he was doing, and standing for, was right. At that time he had absolutely the right 'brand' to face the enemy.

So, how are you being perceived by others? The sub-text in that question is "How are you being referred to by others?" How do your family, friends and workmates refer to you? How do they perceive you? As the funniest person they know? As the most beautiful? Or the richest? It is generally your characteristics that will have built your current personal brand. Your job, your appearance, your achievements, your interests, your skills set, your capabilities, how you live your life and where, all play a major role in how you are perceived.

We have a Home Secretary in Great Britain who is proposing to bring in individual ID cards. He says he wants them for security reasons, but imagine if we could use them for our individual branding purposes. Would you have one by choice? If you did, what extra words would you like to put on your personal ID Card: Professional? Trustworthy? Reliable? Approachable? Charitable? Famous? A Jolly Good Sort?! Does your own personal brand shout those things or do you think it would be easier to have a card with your own virtues written on it? How convenient it would be! - you could just hand it out to prevent others from making erroneous judgements about you and your character.

People do make erroneous judgements about us simply by what we project. Images are being beamed out of us all the time and an indelible picture is being formed by the people we meet. Is it the picture we want to be perceived or would we like to have some say about it? Of course we would!

To achieve the right brand takes insight, knowledge and strategic intention, and if you think that being 'branded' as an individual is distasteful, please think again. Developing your own brand is not about being flashy, although some people do take it to extremes. If you think for one minute that you are too small to make an impact, try going to bed with a mosquito in the room! If you don't blow your own trumpet and market yourself, no-one else will. Build your brand with truth, dignity, honesty and without cynicism.

However, build on your existing brand with care - make sure that what you are building is strategically what you want. You may want to shed some of your less attractive traits along the way through in-depth personal analysis. Changing a well-developed, less-than-perfect brand can be a long, hard struggle.

Non-verbal communication (NVC), or image, is at the core of our personal brand, acting as a visual shorthand and hopefully showing us at our best. NVC should show you in your very best light and help to influence others' first perception of you in as positive a way as possible. It is well known that your first impression on others is made within the first 10-20 seconds. People quickly form opinions about your economic level, educational level, trustworthiness, your social position, level of sophistication, social and educational heritage, success in present and current endeavours, moral character, future possibilities and even whether they like you! We all do it and this vital first impression can make the difference between clinching a contract or not. Make a bad impression and your influence over events can slip away.

Successful people generally look successful: they wear clothes that look attractive, they are well-groomed, they speak clearly and carry themselves with confidence. The image that comes across is that they feel good about themselves and can interact well and influence others. They have rapport—the magic element that we sometimes find so elusive.

To summarise, Personal Branding works, but we need to understand that the whole process is driven by intentional strategies. This process of branding makes an indelible impression on others about you and the nature of your business. It will help you gain a good reputation, acceptance by your clients and move you towards achieving your goals.

### So what is a great personal brand?
A great personal brand is a recognisable precise identity in an individual that promotes their overall skills, qualities and values. This will lead to greater credibility, a more defined USP, and will build loyalty leading to further and improved market opportunities. It is the best asset you have. YOU. **ID-YOU©**.

However, it is also a perception or emotion maintained by somebody other than you, that describes the total experience of having a relationship with you. It is important to remember that your brand exists in their mind, just as their brand exists in your mind.

### Why develop a Personal Brand?
It is possible that you or people in your company have recently graduated from university or college, or you may have been working alone or within a company for many years. Do you think you have the competitive edge because you have a good education or great relative experience in your particular field? Well, you might be in for a shock. You may be extremely good at your job, but having a great Personal Brand, understanding what you stand for and presenting yourself immaculately and appropriately are paramount to achieve real success. This isn't just about being 'suited and booted'; not all professions require this, but appropriateness is essential in order to match your client. If his is a dress-down company, he would probably be quite happy to meet you in your smart casual wear; you should just look 'business ready'. However, being dressed less powerfully than your client can put both of you on the back foot: more of this later.

People who are successful generally look it. They wear the right business clothing, they are well-groomed and carry themselves with great confidence (we are not speaking 'brash' here). They can easily build rapport because they understand exactly what that means and they reflect their client and make him feel that his vested interests are at the heart of the conversation. It's a giving thing that comes across as generous, honest and capable, and all this comes within the developed Personal Brand.

Within a company ethos, Personal Branding becomes a huge asset. After all, a company is only as good as its people, so where the concept of personal branding is understood and accepted, every person's own brand within that corporation can be set to echo corporate values. This will grow the company through its people, so that, ultimately, it will be perceived as more professional, capable, trustworthy and achieve positive differentiation over competitors by putting its competitors on the back foot. Individuals then work in a more entrepreneurial way and create greater differentiation from the competition.

James Speros, Chief Marketing Officer, Ernst and Young, USA said this:

*"A company that embraces personal branding as part of their culture allows their management a greater knowledge of people's abilities and therefore greater control and the ability to plan and implement initiatives. On the employee side, it allows individuals to gain recognition for what they do well and move up the career ladder based on their performance, rather than on politics".*

With the building blocks for an effective personal brand in place, the benefits are myriad:

- People will think of you first. You will have 'first thought' status, people will think of you first because you will have the personal brand they require: after all, people buy people and like a good personal interaction. They will also recognise your expertise and integrity.
- Because you are perceived this way, your authority and confidence in your decisions is increased because you are perceived to have the expertise needed and to be the leader in your field.
- This confidence in your expertise will put you in a leadership role and then
- Prestige is enhanced: this puts you in a powerful position and you can
- Improve your earning potential both personally and corporately.
- Others will be attracted to your success, so you will build more contacts and more business.
- Added value will be perceived in what you are selling as you are acknowledged to be the 'expert': people will like what you do and how you do it through the brand you present.
- It may be that your expertise will become a 'hot topic' which even further adds to your prestige.

- Communication will be improved: because of your status, people are more likely to listen than talk.
- Finally and not least, you will earn recognition and this whole book is about recognition—anonymity is not the result you are looking for here!

In order to achieve these benefits, you should start to develop your Personal Brand as a tool. Think of yourself as a 'product'. Then, once formed, you can use your brand as a tool to achieve your individual goals, but you must constantly reinforce the perception you are developing to keep the brand consistent.

## Propel the Image

Ask yourself this. If quality walks through the door, how does it look? If the person in sight is poorly groomed, wearing badly fitting clothing, down at heel shoes and their hair is unkempt and nails grubby, would you regard that as a 'quality' look? Would you be filled with confidence? Obviously not, so constant and consistent detailed attention to the way you present yourself will make an enormous difference to the way you are perceived in the first vitally important seconds. Your promotional chances will effectively increase with a great Personal Brand.

## Determining Your Brand

An important element in determining your Personal Brand is where you want it to be placed. In which arena are you going to achieve the best exposure? Which people can use their influence on your behalf? How do you influence the influencers? The answer is by being what they see as a great brand and being able to deliver what you promise in your arena. So, ask yourself where in your arena can you be seen to have 'first thought' status, expertise, valuable information and a great network?

It is worth remembering that if you develop a reputation within your specialist arena, for whatever expertise it is that you have, it will be broadcast outside that arena as well and your influence will grow along with your integrity.

If the Personal Brand that you develop has the potential to work outside your immediate sphere, don't turn down opportunities to take advantage of that positioning as you will gather momentum and grow your reputation. Develop your brand onwards and outwards to achieve more and more personal success.

As I write these words, the Forbes Top 10 Celebrities Listing is as follows:

- ☆ Oprah Winfrey
- ☆ Tiger Woods
- ☆ Mel Gibson,
- ☆ George Lucas
- ☆ Shaquille O'Neal
- ☆ Steven Spielberg
- ☆ Johnny Depp
- ☆ Madonna
- ☆ Elton John
- ☆ Tom Cruise

Oprah has been on this list for years now. She has done an amazing job with her Personal Brand, but she still keeps a lot of her brand discreet and only shows the world what she wants to show. This is great branding, as she keeps her integrity through keeping her private life private.

The great majority of us will never reach this height of Personal Branding, and we may not wish to. A great Personal Brand doesn't necessarily mean being famous but means having integrity in whatever it is you do. You can develop your brand along strong guidelines and check as you go by referring back to these guidelines whenever you feel you may be losing track. Think of the following 6 points and develop your brand along these lines.

## 1. Personality

You are unique, and it is your own DNA strands that make you what you are. From this, over the years, has developed your own unique personality and it is this magnet that will attract the buyers to your Personal Brand.

They relate to you and what you believe. This is where, if you have the ability, you can build a strong rapport with your client base, so that they will enjoy working with you. You may even find that you have more in common with your clients than you thought, so a little research into what they enjoy may well reveal another commonly held interest that you can work alongside.

Your honest self-appraisal is also a healthy and clean attitude when dealing with clients. They like to believe that you have flaws and that you are not 'perfect': admitting these flaws draws them to you and once again, builds the rapport that is such a big part of your Personal Brand. This links well with the next point - differentiation.

## 2. Differentiation

Your USP should stand out and be noticed as a specialism that you have developed and where you are recognised as the best within your arena. Look at David Beckham, for example, a great soccer player who is not only a skilled player but who also has the ability to motivate and unite the side he plays for, whether it is as England's captain or when playing for 'Real Madrid'. This uniqueness and specialism has led him to huge success in other fields; he is the face of sunglasses, aftershaves and jewellery as well as a representative of numerous clothing brands. But David Beckham hasn't tried to be anything other than a great footballer. This enables his fans to know more about him and see more of him doing what he does best. Thus his value increases in the marketplace as he represents further products who benefit from his status. He has kept his image relatively clean despite media attempts to 'unseat the king'.

It is only natural to want to be as successful as possible, but it is better to be a specialist than 'all things to all people' as this only dilutes your message and your brand.

So how can you make the most of your particular skills set? Get to know your arena intimately. Then use simple marketing techniques on yourself – on **ID-YOU**© – to get out to sell.

- You should have great referrals to show.
- Your goals and visions should be achievable and interesting to others.
- You should be the most famous professional in your industry.

- You can do it better than your competition—what is it that sets you apart from them?
- Be single minded in your intent and develop your Personal Brand like a razor!
- You should have great strength of character, be known as a listener, a great speaker or that you have a talent for achieving the unachievable!
- You can do what no-one else can do, your skills are highly niched.

## 3. 'First Thought' Status

You will be the one every person thinks of to solve issues when they are faced with a particular challenge. People need to know you exist, and if you have built your reputation well, you will be visible.

Perhaps you might win an award for your expertise. There are many out there, industrial awards, lifetime awards, (MBE, CBE, etc), writing awards, or simply 'best employee' corporate awards. All leading to your being in a place where people are aware of your potential and your brand.

## 4. Memorability

You must be memorable. How can you be remembered if you don't make an impression? Don't investigate the 'safe ground', make your mark and don't remain anonymous even if this means turning some people off by your branding. You cannot please all the people all of the time and you can be sure that whatever it is you are offering will simply be embraced more by those people who really understand what you are trying to offer.

Your overall Personal Brand will be built using many strands. Later in this book, I will detail the physical part of your brand, what you wear, how you wear it and its appropriateness, but there are also the 'invisibles' that make up **ID-YOU**©. The kind of life you live, where you live it and how well-known you are in doing just that, plus the general behaviour you exhibit—your sense of humour, the way you deal with people and your emotional responses to situations. I will also discuss voice and clarity of voice in later chapters and how you handle personal space zones, all these things can spoil a brand if they are not well developed.

## 5. Integrity

You should always do what you promise, and be seen to have high values and strong personal beliefs. This is the bedrock of your brand and will lead to the influence you need. People choose people and will often choose to work with someone they truly like more than the most talented person. If they can see that you will always deliver what they expect and in the manner they expect, your integrity will rise and your brand will shine. You will also feel good about it.

## 6. Continuity

Keep on doing what's working. Always work on the visibility of your brand— if it's not seen, you won't be noticed! You may have the best product and the best team, but if no-one knows you are out there you may as well pack up and go home. Always be ready for an opportunity: be proactive rather than reactive.

## What Does a Good Brand Engender?

In the United States, the average person is exposed to more than 3000 brand messages each day! And that total is growing. Across all categories research shows that people will pay 9%-12% more for a brand they know and trust than for unfamiliar ones. This applies as much to your own personal brand as to well known products such as Hoover or Boots the Chemists. Coca-Cola's brand is estimated to be worth about half the company's total market value!

A good brand engenders strong emotional responses in others and with thought and care you can develop your Personal Brand to be perceived as strongly as you wish—look at how pop culture throws up extraordinary individuals and how film stars develop their own personal brands to enhance their careers.

These strong emotional responses will decide whether:

>    YOU ARE TRUSTED OR NOT
>    YOU ARE LIKED OR NOT
>    YOU ARE REMEMBERED OR NOT

and finally whether

> YOU ARE VALUED OR NOT.

## On a Personal Level – Who Buys You?

There are three reasons why someone buys you, your product or your services, and they all provide the client with confidence and peace of mind:

1. YOU APPEAR HONEST

    People think they can trust you and that you will always handle yourself and your clients in a trustworthy and honest manner.

2. YOU APPEAR KNOWLEDGEABLE

    People feel you know what you are saying and doing, and they can rely on your expertise.

3. YOU APPEAR SINCERE

    People believe that you have their vested interests at heart and that you will ensure that the work you do for them will be done with the client's targets and wishes as paramount.

If you can keep these qualities integral to your personal brand you will develop your clients' trust and integrity in you and your services. Lose touch with them and you lose your integrity *and* your clients.

# Notes

## Chapter Two

*"The person who says it cannot be done
should not interrupt the person doing it"* Chinese Proverb

### Suit the 21st Century

Being current is an important part of having a good professional image. This doesn't mean that you have to be a fashion victim, far from it; an over-trendy appearance won't give an impression of a sharp mind, nor will a dated dress sense. If you wear clothes that show you are really aware of the economic and social climate, you will be seen as in tune with modern trends both in business and in your personal life. Again, it is the perception of you by others and your appropriateness to your particular industry that will effectively build your own Personal Brand.

You can choose to manage your appearance cost-effectively, with style and ease, but if you let it get out of hand you may eventually have to deal with it as a form of crisis management. I will show you presently how your appearance is your 'first impression' method of communication. You will be presenting to the world a map of the person within. You can't possibly represent everything about yourself in a few seconds, but people will surmise a whole lot about you from those first vital moments. As far as they are concerned, perception is reality.

- What do you want that communication to say?
- What don't you want it to say?!
- What is your environment?
- Who is your audience, and
- What is their expectation?

Be aware that, in a business environment, being too far ahead of the times is inappropriate. Although there is now less insistence on very formal office clothing and a more widespread adoption of casual clothes, to adopt these in an inappropriate manner will put you at a disadvantage, not to mention the organisation that you are representing.

In summary, any individual or organisation that ignores the reality of 'personal' branding does so at their peril. Let's look at some examples:

- An individual may have huge potential for promotion on performance, but the company feels that his/her indifference to dress and grooming will do more harm than good for the corporate image.
- The sales force of a competitor has started to improve the appearance of its team and it becomes obvious that unless you do the same you will lose your market share.
- After a company take-over, unifying the two workforces in a seamless fashion can be achieved through the personal branding of the new entity's people.
- A fast-growing company with a regular intake of graduates wants to ensure that their new people from the very start are well versed in understanding their own Personal Brand values and see the importance of professional presentation at all times.
- The introduction of dress-down Friday in a particular company hasn't been altogether successful but the company would like, whilst maintaining team morale, to continue the more relaxed code without the danger of their people becoming sloppy. Taking note of the individual brands within this company can develop a better team spirit and a more entrepreneurial attitude.

Getting the right response from others ultimately depends on each individual taking responsibility for their own brand values.

## First Impressions Count!

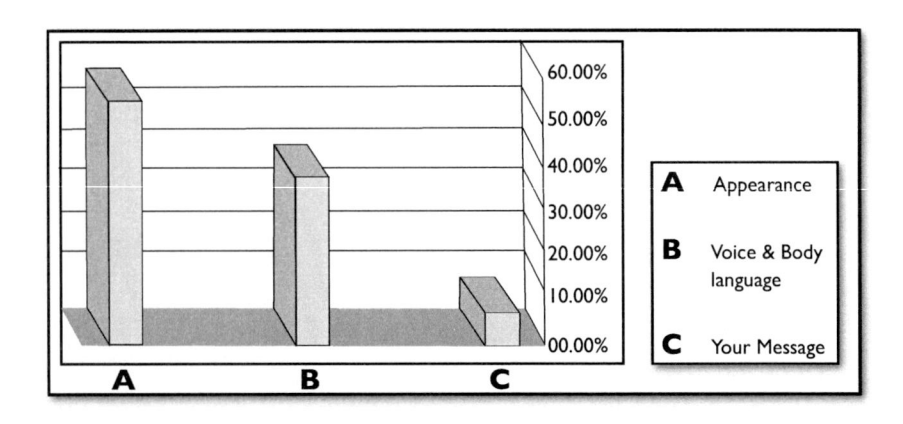

| | % |
|---|---|
| A Appearance | 60.00% |
| B Voice & Body language | 40.00% |
| C Your Message | 10.00% |

- On arrival you will be judged in approximately 10 –20 seconds!
- Appearance and body language account for 55% of your first impression.
- Voice alone accounts for 38% of your first impression.
- Your message, or what you have to say, accounts for only 7% of your total impression! So get the first 93% wrong, and it is highly likely that no-one is listening to you.
- Style + Substance = POSITIVE IMPACT

## How Are My First Impressions?

### Handshake

- Crusher?
- Wet Fish
- Limp Lily?
- Firm?
- Dominant?

A crushing handshake is over-dominant between men and frankly painful for most women to receive, especially if rings are being ground between fingers by the pressure!

A damp handshake, a Wet Fish (!), is most unpleasant. Unfortunately, some people do suffer from sweaty hands and you should be careful about this. Have a tissue or a handkerchief available (out of sight) to dry your hands. If you know you are going to be asked to meet people, spray your palm with anti-perspirant immediately beforehand. In severe cases, there is a minor operation that can be undertaken to diminish sweating hands.

The Limp Lily can imply that you are weak.

Ladies, don't be afraid to shake hands firmly with people; gentlemen, you shouldn't weaken your handshake too much when shaking hands with a woman.

A double-handed handshake is thought to show sincerity but, at least in the UK, people don't feel entirely comfortable with this – it's a bit over the top.

Ask for feedback from family and friends and be prepared to work on it. Ask them how you come across from the following pointers:

### Body Language—Posture
- Am I Poised?
- Slouched?
- Easy?
- Confident?
- Slumped?
- Taut?

There are some great organisations out there to help you with your posture if you are having problems with it. The Alexander Technique, Yoga and Pilates are exercise regimes that can be easily sourced and can make a significant difference to your posture and your well-being.

### Body Language—Facial Expressions
- Do I smile easily?
- Do I rarely smile in business situations?
- I'm aware that my teeth could be better, so I don't smile much
- I'm not a smiley person!

Practise in front of a mirror! If you are concerned about teeth, visit your local dentist at least once a year and your hygienist every 6 months: you will reap the benefit! A smile is rewarded.

### Body Language – Eye Contact
- Do I find it hard to maintain direct eye contact?
- I find eye contact easy
- Do I blink quite frequently?
- I wear darkened lenses so eye contact doesn't matter

Become aware of your eye contact and practise it—good eye contact doesn't mean staring hard at someone, just looking and listening and gesturing by nodding or smiling to show that you are involved with the conversation. If you look away or over someone's shoulder, they will feel that you are not engaged with them and that makes the speaker feel uncomfortable. Unless you must wear them, darkened lenses shouldn't be worn as good eye contact is hugely diminished by these and the wearer is perceived as 'hiding' him/herself.

### Style – What are my feelings about my working wardrobe?
- I don't need to dress up for work
- I can wear anything to work
- I like to put on my work clothes
- I have to be 'suited and booted' for work
- I like to be appropriate at work
- I have a classic style
- I have a modern, trendy style
- I work in a creative environment so business clothes are unusual
- I like to be 'business ready'.
- I don't know what is really expected of me at work.

### Shoes
- I keep my shoes clean and well repaired
- My shoes are a little dated
- I like expensive shoes
- I like lots of shoes
- I'd rather be comfortable than stylish
- I like the latest trends in shoes
- (Women) I wear very high heels at work
- (Women) I wear open-toe shoes to work

### Personal Grooming – ask yourself which of the following matter to you;
- I don't bother much at work
- (Women) I always wear some make-up at work
- (Women) I never wear make-up
- (Men) I don't always shave on dress-down days
- I never wear stained clothes or clothes in disrepair
- I think excellent personal grooming is essential

- (Women) I always keep spare tights in a drawer at work
- I always keep an emergency repair kit in a drawer at work
- I shower every day
- I always use deodorant
- I have a regular appointment at the hairdressers
- I have a regular appointment at the hygienist/dentist
- I keep my nails manicured
- I take care of my skin

## Clarity and Tone of Voice – do people really hear you well?
- My voice is soft
- People always hear me well
- My pronunciation is well paced
- My accent is distinctive
- I tend to mumble
- I talk too fast sometimes
- I can be loud
- I could do with a variation in pitch
- My voice is rather high

There is more on 'voice' in the following pages.

## Conversational skills – practice makes perfect
- I find it easy to talk to people
- People tell me I'm easy to talk to
- I find small talk very difficult
- I'm rather shy talking to strangers
- Networking occasions are a nightmare for me
- I feel really at home at a networking event

## Physical Fitness
- What's that?
- I don't have time to exercise
- I visit the gym often

- I get breathless climbing the stairs
- I smoke

Physical fitness is obviously one of life's most important things and time should be taken out of your day to spend at least half an hour doing some physical activity to make the heart beat faster to develop stamina and to strengthen your muscles and joints. Of course not everyone is able to do this. The wheelchair-bound and physically-disabled need to build their own brands as much as the next person. If you are disabled then you have to work on those values that make you interesting and memorable as much as, if not more than, an able-bodied person.

### Memory – this does need stimulation to keep working well!
- I always forget people's names
- I need to write lists as an aide memoire
- I have given someone the wrong name!
- I have a special way of remembering names

There are specialists who can teach memory skills. It is worth investing in some further reading on this subject. I use memory tags to remember people's names—when introduced to someone try to repeat their name in your head and use it as often in the following conversation as you can without being ridiculous! Try to think of their name as a colour, or an object, or an animal, or anything that that name reminds you of and then when you will see them again that thought should trigger their name. Once again, practice will make perfect.

### Colours
- I have no idea what colour suits me
- I am quite conservative in choosing colours
- I always choose neutrals that are 'safe'
- I'd like to be flattered by colours that suit me
- I wear bright colours often
- I mostly wear black
- Turn to the colour pages and learn more!

## Voice Impact
Be aware of the clarity, strength, modularity, pace and pitch of your voice

## Clarity
Your voice needs to be clear, otherwise people will simply switch off and become bored with trying to hear you. Keep your head up, breathe well and speak from the diaphragm, not from your throat. Articulate clearly.

## Strength
The strength of your voice will come from your breathing as much as your vocal chords. If you are planning to begin presenting and public speaking often, then it would be advisable to take professional voice lessons with an expert who can teach you the techniques for developing a stronger and more lasting voice. A voice that is not strong can appear weak and ineffective.

## Modularity
Listening to a flat-paced, flat-toned speech is dull and enervating. So be aware of adding liveliness to your voice, adding rises and falls in strength and pace, giving it a rhythm of tone that stimulates the listener and makes them interested and you interesting.

## Pace and Pitch
Keep the pace of your voice lively and upbeat, but never speak too quickly as this will again lose the listeners' interest. You can vary the pace by slowing down in 'emotional' or 'expressive' moments and then picking it up again. If, for example, you are telling an exciting story, this will lead you to increase the pitch and tone when relevant and lower it again when more subdued.

## Accents
Accents can be a great asset to your Personal Brand and can add cachet. It distinguishes you from others and makes you unique. Janet Street Porter, Cilla Black and Jonathan Ross have developed their USP from their accents. However, do be sure that your accent is not so regional as to be incomprehensible to those listening!

## Interest

You just know when you are listening to a great speech. It holds you in its thrall and is fascinating. A skilled orator will use all the above elements to stimulate your interest and keep you listening. Be sure that your speech is relevant to your audience, too.

**Notes**

To improve and move on I will …

Date:_____

# CHAPTER THREE

# VISIONS AND GOALS

## WHAT IS YOUR VISION?

The dictionary describes vision as 'great perception, especially of future developments'. This is what you need in order to grow your brand. You have to know what you are aiming to achieve, to do, to experience, whether in the short or long term, in order to build your brand to fit your vision. You should also believe passionately in this vision—half measures are no good! Every great man/woman had a vision and you must focus on your own vision every day to keep you on target. Edison made thousands of experiments before he achieved the fulfilment of his vision and produced his light bulb: it was his unique character that kept him on target. This total belief in his idea was his 'Unique Selling Point' (USP) that set him apart and kept him working on his theories.

Seeing your Vision clearly will enable you to build your USP to achieve what you want. You will be able to differentiate yourself from your competition—remember, "anonymity is not the goal here"!

Don't confuse Vision with Goals. Your Vision is the BIG PICTURE, the place you ultimately want to be and the experiences you will have at a given time in the future.

## WHAT ARE YOUR GOALS?

Your Goals will be those steps you take along the way to reach your Vision. Setting your goals in the right order and reaching them step-by-step is the only way to achieve your Vision. Do this to start with in the short term, year by year. Write yourself an action plan:

"By the end of 200? I will have achieved …" (write what you want to achieve), By the end of 200? I will have achieved …" (write the next goal etc., etc.)

You can then see how these steps will lead to more middle term goal achievement, in say 3 years. And all this will lead to the ultimate goal, say 7 years or more away, and the fulfilment of your Vision.

Your Personal Brand will help you along the route to your Vision. Building it with your future Goals and Vision in mind will make it more achievable and successful.

### BUILD A MISSION STATEMENT

If your goal is to build a recognisable brand within your expertise and gain visibility, or to be recognised as a high profile personality, then you should understand how important your influence over this has to be. It is who you are, what you say and what you do that matters. The most important thing about having your personal brand is that it is about 'being yourself with honesty'. We all recognise individuals we have met with a magnetic charisma, for whom opportunities seem to arrive at the drop of a hat and who you feel are completely at ease with themselves. These people have already set about them their own brand values and are broadcasting them to the world in their most honest and authentic manner.

Think of your brand as your DNA. You were born with a unique DNA, shared with no-one else in the whole world. What you are about to develop with a personal brand of your own is like that DNA, something that you can shape and develop with integrity to create distinction and differentiation from everyone else.

So, do you really know yourself? Do you know what you want to achieve—the goals and ultimate vision for your life? You will be relieved to know that I am not going to delve into the deeper meaning of life, the Universe and everything, but in order to take the idea of a personal brand and develop it fully, you will first need to know yourself.

You are the sum of your intellectual property that has been developing since birth. Now you are going to advertise this property to help you achieve your vision and help others see what you have to offer, your strengths, resources and wisdom that will set out your USP and make you remarkable.

So what is your USP? Build a simple mission statement that sets you apart from the rest. This will also express the benefits that others will gain from working with you, and is built on your strengths and the specific values that you are offering. It should be compelling and easily communicable.

### Try the following exercise:

Hand out to approximately a dozen trusted friends and business associates an s.a.e. enclosing a questionnaire that asks them the following questions. Tell them they can answer anonymously if they prefer (which is probably better) and say that you would like their opinions to be objective and not necessarily kind!

- What three succinct adjectives would they use to describe you?
- How would they describe you, and what you do, to people who don't know you?
- What sets you apart from your competition?
- Do they think you have a USP? If so, what is it?

Now do a SWOT analysis on yourself (Strengths, Weaknesses, Opportunities and Threats). Analyse these as objectively as you can and compare the results with the replies you receive from your questionnaire.

From this you can find keywords that could become part of your business brand and mission statement, and that you can ascribe to yourself as being the core of your own personal brand.

For example:
Your own self-description: Professional, Caring, Dynamic

Others' description of you: Insightful, Flexible, Forward-thinking.

Your USP: 20 years of expertise in the field, market leader, added values.

### Example Statement:

"A market leader with 20 years of expertise, combining a professional and forward thinking attitude with a flexible, insightful and caring style of interpersonal relationship management".

*Visions and Goals*

What you are looking to achieve here is a short message people will remember when they think about you, one that enhances your own personal brand.

In the appendix to this book you will find an additional article by leading expert Jonathan Stanley on how to choose and define your own values.

### INTERNAL AND EXTERNAL OBJECTIVES

*"Too many people overvalue what they are not and undervalue what they are".* Malcolm S. Forbes

To get started, ask yourself "What are my core values?" and whether you have visited them lately!

Q.1 "What really does matter to me?"

Q.2 "How do I want to be perceived?"

### 1. "WHAT REALLY MATTERS TO ME?"

Have you considered this recently? It is a huge part of your personal brand. Choose some words to help you, e.g. Visibility, Status, Freedom, Integrity, Financial success, Security, Challenge, etc....

I can't overstate how important this is in building your Personal Brand. Find your top three adjectives and ask yourself whether you are projecting those values to the community you work and live in? Does that community, be it a business or social one, recognise those overt values in you?

### 2. "HOW DO I WANT TO BE PERCEIVED?"

How are you coming across? With integrity, professionalism, capability and rapport? As an authentic and charismatic person worthy of respect?

Again, take some words to help you, e.g. Professional, Confident, Amusing, Warm, Elegant, Dynamic, Approachable, a good listener etc. If you find this difficult, think about the values and characteristics you look for, and admire, in other people.

When you have picked your top three, think about whether you are achieving this wish? If you chose Professional, Warm, and Approachable, do you think that you're being recognised as being really professional, that people find you easy to talk to and that you have the warmth you think you do? You may think that you are being perceived in a certain way, but double check, do the exercise from the preceding page. You may be surprised: after all, it is what other people think of you that builds your brand, not what you think you are.

Once you have evaluated and defined your core values, know what you stand for and have mapped those values to build your brand, you must follow it up with consistency of behaviour: without consistency your integrity will be lost. It takes years to build integrity, but a second to lose it by not acting consistently—the trust will be gone.

### Developing a Strategy

Building your brand doesn't happen overnight. It takes belief in your vision and application.

What you should have above all is integrity, which in turn will lead to your being perceived as having your clients' and/or work colleagues' best interests at heart.

You should be perceived as being honest and capable, you should match your clients both in intention, body language, behaviour and style and they should feel that you know what they need and that you will address it professionally.

Your own personal brand is like having your very own trademark, where people recognise what they are going to get and how it will be delivered. If you want to be eccentric—maybe your market is outrageous entertainment!—fine, so long as that is what the customer wants and knows it is what he will get. How can you expect people to remember you if you are not memorable?

Coco Chanel said,

**"In order to be irreplaceable one must always be different"**.

I recently worked with a man who for years had owned his own company, but worked entirely in the back-room on IT and admitted he had no idea of how to be the Managing Director. However, he won a huge contract for his software and suddenly needed to front his organisation as Managing Director and 'match' his clients. After our consultation and a shopping trip together, he was transformed.

The letter I received from him about his reception at home and at work made my day: he was no longer 'Mr. Beige'; his colleagues at work said he now had gravitas and was changed out of all recognition. But top of the list of benefits that they saw was that their company was now being perceived as 'seriously professional' and the deals were coming in thick and fast. His personal brand was now that of the company (and vice versa) and the company ethos had direction and form.

A personal brand is not about being famous, it is about having influence. People in all walks of life manipulate their brands to their advantage. Let's look at some examples of people who have changed their look and style to a great extent.

### Diana, Princess of Wales

Remember those early photographs of the young Diana, living in Kensington, working in a nursery, the see-through summer skirt and the shaggy hair-style that hid her eyes? How about the engagement photographs in the blue suit with the pie crust collar, peplum jacket, and long full skirt? Did she look confident and aware, or timid and insecure? The latter I think, but look what happened: she married the Prince of Wales and came out of the shadows. She decided that she wanted to be more her own woman, and it is tempting to surmise that she took a lot of style advice.

Her whole look became much more tailored to suit her particular figure, her hair was cut in a sharp style to suit her angular features, she had great legs and showed them off with knee length skirts and high heels. Suddenly she became not just a 'person in her own right', but an absolute fashion icon. There was a cult of personality built around her and she was never again just a consort. She had a fantastic personal brand that has survived her death.

## Margaret Thatcher

In her early years, Mrs. Thatcher was soft looking, and softly spoken, with an old-fashioned hair-style, and frankly, dowdy clothes. As her intellect and political skill took her further up the governmental ladder, the image changed. Her voice, having become quite strident, was toned down, her teeth were 'improved', her hair was coloured in a soft tone and swept over to the side in a much more gentle fashion. She wore beautifully tailored, but simple suits with brooches pinned high up on her shoulder (which raises the eye level, and therefore gives an impression of height).

Her handbag was a feature: it became a 'power' handbag as it seemed to grow bigger and bigger! She clearly had media instruction on body language and the do's and don'ts of appearing on television, in interviews and at conferences. You were far more likely to see her holding her hands together, with her head on one side, listening and then gently admonishing her interviewer, rather than wagging her fingers at them like a head mistress as she used to do. Do you think she took some branding advice? I do.

## Michael Foot and Tony Blair

Do you remember the photos of Michael Foot, the one time leader of the Labour Party? The downtrodden working man seemed to be epitomised by his scruffy, 'couldn't give a toss' look. Compare that with the New Labour Party headed by the elegant and cool, (if lately somewhat distrusted) Tony Blair—yes, the political image-makers do have a lot to answer for, whatever your party leanings might be.

## Madonna

Earlier in this book you will have seen that, in the Forbes Top 10 Celebrities, Madonna's position was No.8. What has kept her at the top of the charts for such a long time? Here is an absolute chameleon of an entertainer, with her brand as an entertainer the building block of her 'product'. She changes the 'packaging' of her product every time she issues a new CD: she never looks the same on two album covers. This is a clever use of brand manipulation, appearing 'fresh' and 'different' each time she appears, whether it is on the cover of a CD or in person in concert.

There are multiple examples of personal branding around us every day. Pick up the paper and see who is in the news now, whether it is for good reasons (or not) and think about what their personal brand has achieved for them (or not).

## PACKAGING THE PRODUCT

The major part of personal branding is wardrobe and later I shall discuss this in more detail, but first, draw yourself a pie chart. Look at the way you live your life, and what are the most important parts of it. Do you spend more time at work, say 5 days a week from 9-5.30 or even longer? Then your wardrobe should reflect this proportion. Are you a working parent? Look at how much time is spent at work and how much with your children and, again, divide the wardrobe spend accordingly. How much time do you spend entertaining/ being entertained, and how much time on leisure activities etc. Maybe you don't work at all, but feel that your look is just as important to you—so go for it!

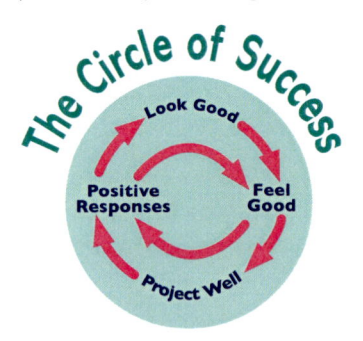

This is the Circle of Success. Starting at 12 o'clock, if you look good, you feel good, and because you feel good you present a better image of yourself to the world. This is then returned by good responses from the people you encounter, which reinforces the effect and leaves you feeling even better. This is commonly called the halo effect, a good image bringing confidence about ability (true or not!). The alternative circle is destructive. Imagine that you don't look your best, you lack confidence and feel uncomfortable in company so you feel awkward. This is then reinforced by poor responses from people, and you end up feeling worse than ever. A reverse downward spiral is starting. People will often not bother to look for the talent inside an uninspiring person.

Try to keep this Circle of Success in your mind, and aim at looking and feeling good and you will be astonished by the improvement in the responses to you. Shoulders back, smile!

In 1931 Fay Weldon wrote:

*"Every time you open your wardrobe, you look at your clothes and you wonder what you are going to wear. What you are really saying is "Who am I going to be today?"."*

## DRESSING DOWN DILEMMAS

Whether to dress in a formal way for work or to take the more casual dress-down option is often a problem for businesses. Whatever is decided it should be appropriate for the business and its clients. It is not sensible to put yourself on the back foot by being dressed down for a client meeting when the client arrives in full bib and tucker! It can also misfire by making him feel uncomfortable, too, so do check with secretaries to see what the dress code will be for meetings out of your office, and always have a suit or at least a jacket and tie hanging in an office cupboard so that you are not caught out too badly when an unexpected client arrives.

Think about the following points:

- Do you ever have to apologise to a client for the way you are dressed? This is a bad way to start a meeting and excuses don't really mend the situation.
- Have you ever decided not to go to a meeting because you haven't got suitable clothes to wear? Again, just remember to keep something at hand in the office to avoid this problem.
- Gentlemen, do you always shave for work and ladies do you always wear some make-up, or do you sometimes decide not to bother?

- Would you be happy to go to work in jeans? Some companies allow this, especially the creative ones, but be sure it is appropriate for your client if a meeting should crop up.
- Do you really know what 'smart casual' means? The company should have a code to which you can ascribe and it should be clear what is meant by smart casual as opposed to 'dress down'. Raised eyebrows from the boss aren't what you need to see!

It is vital to realise how much you can compromise your personal power at work by not 'toeing the corporate line' when it comes to dressing for work. I am frequently asked to consult with companies who are finding that their people are not projecting the company ethos in the way the company wants, by turning up for meetings and events looking distinctly un-businesslike. This misrepresentation of the company is careless and can only cause damage to staff and corporate image alike.

There is more detail in both the men's and women's sections later in this book.

**Notes**

TO IMPROVE AND MOVE ON I WILL ...














































DATE:_____

## Chapter 4

*"I was going to have plastic surgery until I noticed that the doctor's office was full of portraits of Picasso "* Rita Rudner

## Women's Issues

### Looking the Business

Unlike men who, generally, have less choice than women when it comes to what to wear in the office, there are no real rules for the clothes and accessories you should wear—the only proviso here being that your company doesn't have a specific dress code.

What you wear is part of your personal 'brand' and defines how you want the world to perceive you, and should enhance your image, impact and your personality.

However, you do need to know your personal body type and what colours suit you best. With this knowledge safely tucked away, you can choose those clothes that make you feel good, meet your budget, fit the look (either relaxed or more sharp) are versatile and mix well with other garments in your wardrobe.

What you should aim for is a look that is defined and appropriate for your situation and environment. You must always be well groomed and immaculate. Attention to detail is important and aim to develop a style that demands respect before you say a word!

The days of the 'power suit' have long gone, but suits can still be very serious and tailored and can psychologically perform the job you want them to. The style and colours you wear can affect the way others feel about you, so be aware that you may be sending signals that are closed and dominant when you want to be approachable and amenable. For example a dark navy, buttoned-up suit can be very stern, whereas a mid-toned open style is more friendly.

This kind of style may well be appropriate in some situations, but on the whole a slightly more relaxed look has arrived with more fluid and softer lines. The classic revered and buttoned jacket is still around, but you can also look for edge-to-edge jackets, zipped and collarless styles. You can ring the changes with bright and interesting tops underneath and wear trousers as well as skirts of different lengths to ring the changes.

Alternatives to the classic suit also include dresses, which, if simple, can be varied by adding a jacket, short and neat or longer in style, and fine knits.

Whatever you do, don't overdo the jewellery—10 pieces is an absolute maximum and that is counting both earrings and all rings! Keep it simple, keep it classy. As in make-up, less is always more.

### **AM I CONTEMPORARY? (WOMEN)**

If you are in business it is important that you 'match' your clients, so depending upon your type of business, environment, and personal preferences the safe rule of thumb is to be contemporary and have clothes, shoes and accessories that:

- Aren't too trendy (unless your career is in a 'trendy' industry)
- Complement you both physically and in your personality
- Are appropriate
- Fit well
- Are versatile and work well with other items in your wardrobe
- And above all, are well cared for

It is easy to wreck your image by wearing clothes that are old-fashioned and 'stodgy', which of course refers back to your attitude to business—be aware that old-fashioned dressing can be seen to reflect an old-fashioned approach to business.

Here are some questions to ask yourself about your attitude to fashion, style and your working wardrobe at home:

- When was the last time you had some advice at a beauty counter and tried some innovative new products?

- Are you wearing heavy base foundation and powder? Find the newer, lighter products.
- When was the last time you tried a new hair cut/colour or even a younger, more up-to-date hairdresser?
- Do you always buy from that 'safe' shop in the high street, or do you sometimes take a chance in a stylish boutique for a change?
- Do you own a brass buttoned blazer? Oh dear, only good for golf, rowing regattas and sailing.
- If you open your wardrobe door, do you see mainly black?
- Do you consider matching shoes to belts and handbags?
- How dated are your accessories? When was the last time you bought something to add a flourish to an outfit?
- Could you consider colouring out any grey hairs?
- Do you own navy-blue tights? And navy shoes? Oops.
- Have you tried some of the new styles of smart fitted shirts, worn outside skirts and trousers, with bracelet length sleeves?
- Are there still shoes in the back of your wardrobe that you haven't worn for years?
- Do you consider the proportions of jewellery you are wearing, or whether you might look better in silver rather than gold (or vice-versa) or pearls?
- Do you regularly give yourself a manicure, or better still go to a manicurist?
- How's your undies drawer?! Saggy elastic and grey knicks don't do it as a base for smart clothes!
- Have you considered using the services of a specialist business image consultant?

## GETTING DRESSED (WOMEN)

Do start to enjoy the creative experience of dressing and indulge yourself a little. If you find it difficult to imagine what suits you (and that may be why you have purchased this book), why not tear out as many pictures as you can from magazines where you can see an outfit or a 'look' that you like. Make a collection of these pictures and you will soon begin to see what look is making up the majority of these pictures. Are they more classic than modern, more 'cool' than staid, are there colours that you particularly like? Develop an image of your own that you take pleasure in and that broadcasts your Personal Brand on a consistent basis, an image of comfort in your own fashion sense and style.

Learn to appreciate the selections you have chosen in their colours, textures, patterns and drape. If possible try to purchase one or two outstanding outfits every season, if possible making them complementary to make more use of your expenditure.

Imagine your life-style and work place. If you are employed, dress for the position above your current posting, dress for where you want to be not for where you are. Don't settle for the Southern League when it is the Premier Division you should be shooting for. A well-dressed man or woman makes their mark on their community, their style and radiance is acknowledged. You can do this—it's easy to look great and doesn't have to cost a fortune. Just look around and notice the huge numbers of poorly-dressed men and women who sabotage themselves on a daily basis by 'not bothering'—maybe even in your own office environment. Those of you based in London may like to sit a while in Liverpool Street Station and watch the workers rushing to and fro and all this becomes obvious.

Dress for the body you have, and dress for your lifestyle or the one you wish to attain. Ignore size labels, choose the outfits that fit smoothly over your body without compressing and causing unsightly wrinkles and bulges. Decide what messages you want others to receive and shop for those items of clothing that work best for you and your goals.

Remember though, a wardrobe is always evolving.

## **UNDERSTANDING STYLE, LINE AND PROPORTION (WOMEN)**

We've all got bits we want to hide! Even the most perfect body will dissatisfy its owner somehow, so understanding what you can do to make the most of the good parts you have, and to hide the bits you're not happy with is paramount.

Sunshine or shade? Clever use of 'disguise' dressing will put dubious parts of your body 'in the shade' and good parts 'in the sunshine'. Let me give you an example of this:

Do you remember the wedding of Princess Diana and Charles? Do you remember that dress? A huge meringue of roses and bows and a full skirt gathered onto a waistline . . . waistline? What waistline? Diana, despite her later triumphs, had no waist as such. Despite having a wonderful slim and tall shape, she had a very straight, up and down figure and the worst mistake she made on that amazing day, was to try to show off a non-existent waist. Her figure was undeniably straight and quite boyish. The gathering at the waistline not only didn't give her a waist, it just made her look bulkier (and I'm not even going to go there about the creases!).

Look now, if you will, at the wedding of the Duchess of York who, despite her best efforts, was rarely able to compete with Princess Diana. Yet, on her wedding day she looked absolutely fabulous. Why? She recognised the limitations of her tapered shape and her dress was designed to make the most of it. Gently tapered seaming slimmed her body giving it a svelte, glamorous and chic look. The fitted look was perfect to make the most of her figure and the 'ease' in the garment allowed it to hang elegantly from her shoulders. She looked stunning.

Returning to Princess Diana for a moment—as she came into her own, she had obviously had some style counselling and recognised her own limitations. She worked out hard at the gym and developed stronger shoulders which then gave the illusion of a smaller waist. The clothes she chose were cut to flatter her straight shape, in other words she wore straighter cut shapes with no hint of curves, boxy jackets, sharply pleated or straight skirts and slimline pants and straight-cut jackets. She steered clear of anything curvy, flowery or frilly, and she appeared more elegant and lovely each time we saw her. This is the secret of making the most of a straight figure. If you are more curvy in shape, then you can wear the jackets, dresses and skirts cut with a curve; for example, hold a jacket up on its hanger. Does it have a curved shape from the cut or tailoring? If it does, it will sit well on a tapered or curved or fuller figure, but not well at all on a straight one—it makes sense.

Recognise and support your figure type—you will be surprised with the outcome. The main rule of thumb though is FIT. Too tight clothes that leave a series of rolls across the back, down the sides, and spread buttons across the chest will make you look larger, not smaller. In the elegance stakes, the extra ease in a garment that allows you to move freely will pay dividends.

So ladies, let's begin.

There are invariably four body shapes, and they are all illustrated below:

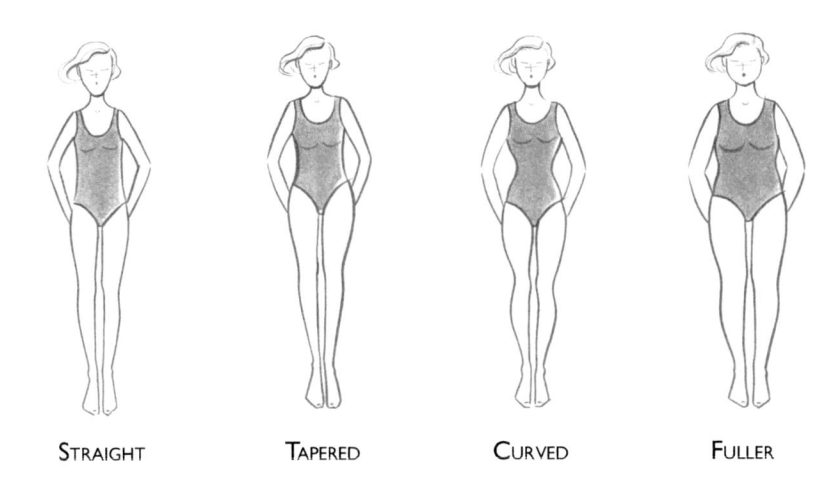

| Straight | Tapered | Curved | Fuller |
|---|---|---|---|

How do you work out which category fits you? There are loads of individual differences between all these figure types, longer legs, shorter legs, narrower shoulders, shorter necks etc. etc., but everyone will fit into a category from the above 4 examples and then define their differences from that starting point.

Curved ladies have definitive waistlines and are broader-hipped, sometimes seeming higher-hipped and can be fuller-busted, although this shape also comes in smaller and petite sizes and is the classic 'model' figure; in larger ladies it becomes the hour-glass figure of Marilyn Monroe and Jane Russell.

If you think you have a 'curved' figure, hold your thumb directly on the bra under the breast, and extend the forefinger to the waistline, you should have a good stretch—in other words you are quite long bodied (see example picture).

The other side of this coin is the tapered or slightly shorter-waisted lady, where if you were to do the previous exercise the gap between thumb and forefinger would be noticeably shorter. This quite often goes with a fuller bust, especially after childbirth, and gives the classic tapered look (see picture). Her proportions are also gently rounded and soft. Later in this chapter I will cover the particular proportional issues that effect all the different figure types.

Straight figures have no obvious waistline, and if you were to run your hands down the sides of the torso, there would be no obvious inward shape at the waist, and the hips would appear high and flat and the legs long and slim, with sometimes quite a flat behind.

The fuller figures are larger versions of any or all of the preceding shapes, and have just grown bigger all around. They may have been 'straight' 'curved' or 'tapered', but with weight gain, or just a predisposition to a heavier frame, can now be recognised as 'fuller' or 'contoured'.

So what? Why do I need to know all this?

If you know and understand your figure shape and any of the limitations that come with it, you will know how to dress that figure to its best advantage. You will 'shop wiser' with knowledge and stop making the buying errors that may leave you with unworn clothes pushed to one side of your wardrobe—an expensive shopping glitch!

It also means that you will have the knowledge to choose the appropriate clothes for your workplace environment, and be seen always to appear smart and well dressed with the self-esteem that subsequently gets you noticed.

How to make the best of your proportions

### CURVED

Lucky ladies you!! This is the perfect shape to be, you can emphasise your waist, which is one of your most feminine features, with belts and fitted outfits that hug the body, feel free to wear whatever suits you best, bearing in mind of course that colour counts here too, and look further down this chapter to find the individual proportional issues that can still arise no matter what shape you have.

### Straight

As you don't have an obvious waist, don't try to make one! Avoid belts and obvious waistlines on clothing. Wear straight cut clothes, boxy jackets, straight and pleated skirts and pants. Straighter figures usually have slim, boyish hips, so make the most of your figure and step out in long line pants, overshirts and straight coats. Remember, avoid all clothes cut with a curve, they will not fit well on your body and will not do you any favours.

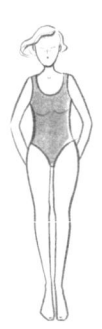

### Tapered

Once again, here it is best not to try to make a waist which will inevitably make you look shorter in the midriff area by drawing attention to it. So avoid belts and choose clothes that skim the body with well-cut 'A' lines and darts. Wear longer line jackets to give you length and, if carrying a little weight, choose single-breasted jackets and clothing with vertical stripes rather than horizontal. A V-neckline will add length to the neck and an illusion of added height and a longer, slimmer body length.

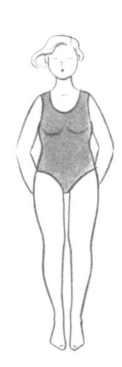

### Fuller

Most ladies who are now described as 'fuller' may previously have been straight, tapered or curved. However, now is the time to use the right proportional skills to lengthen, slim and flatter your shape. Keeping clothing in monotones, i.e. tops, skirts or trousers all the same colour will slim and lengthen. Avoid colour blocks. This happens when, for example, a white top is worn tucked into black pants: this can exaggerate a larger waistline, form unwitting horizontal lines and both widen and shorten the figure. Avoid any shiny fabrics, too, as these catch the light and make you seem larger; stick to matt colours and, in a perfect world, quite dark colours, too. You should also avoid thick, boucle fabrics which bulk out too much

To help with an illusion of height and a slimmer line, wear a long fine scarf around the neck: this will give a long vertical line as well. Avoid double-breasted jackets or cardigans and, once again, make the illusion longer and slimmer by using the buttons on jackets etc. to form a long line down the front of the body. Often, longer than knee-length single-breasted tops over trousers can be a very good look for the larger lady, but only if you are tall; otherwise the look can swamp you.

## ISSUES OF SCALE (WOMEN)

At this point it is just as well to mention issues of scale, as quite often women wear jewellery that is unsuitable for their size. If you are larger than you want to be and wear small-scale jewellery—little earings, little chains around the neck, and small bracelets, these only manage to make you look larger. Be bold! Go for larger pieces, chunky wooden bracelets, larger necklaces and good-sized earings that take attention away from the face: these are in proportion to your size and will consequently make you look smaller.

The opposite applies to petite and very slim people. Wearing large pieces of jewellery only serves to make you look smaller and slimmer as they unbalance your shape. This also applies to handbags as small bags on larger bodies can look over-small. Get in proportion, girls!

### TOO TALL?

Horizontal lines are always a sure-fire way of making you look shorter; wearing medium to low heels is an obvious way to reduce the inches; wide trousers with turn-ups will draw the eye down to the ankles and reduce height. If you wear a contrasting shoe with your stockings or tights they will also serve the same purpose of drawing the eye down. A contrasting belt at the waist also works as a 'divider' and cuts the body in half.

## Too Short?

To add inches, vertical lines will always give an impression of greater height whether they are in a pattern, or actually in the material—a cable for example. Keep shapes slimline and take trousers low over your shoes/boots and wear a high heel, (do not allow the hem of the trousers to wrinkle on the shoe as this will draw attention to your feet and ruin the impression!). Dress in monotones if possible, with skirts and tops, trousers and tops the same colour, and wear matching tights and shoes as well: this all gives an impression of length. If you have the legs, a shorter skirt works well, but don't overdo it in the office! Short hairstyles, too, work better if you want to look taller. Keep all your accessories and patterns on your clothing small to medium scale in proportion with your size. Avoid large hats!

## Necks

### To make necks look longer and slimmer

Low necklines will always make your neck look longer, wearing collars buttoned or rolled high up on the neck will foreshorten it even further. However, open-necked shirts and blouses give a good illusion of length. V-necked collarless jackets also help to lengthen a shorter neck. If you wear a scarf, then tying it lower down will lengthen the look.

### To shorten or widen your neck

Polo necks, and scarves tied around the neck cowboy-fashion hide a long neck very well. Upturned collars and either Nehru or Mandarin collars work in your favour, too.

## Shoulders

### To widen narrow shoulders
Shoulder pads are not just an 80's phenomenon, and now, scaled down a great deal, they are great to add width to clothes, giving more stature to shoulders and therefore less attention to the neck. As a bonus, this also makes the waistline seem smaller. Other detailing on the shoulders, such as pleating, will also distract the eye. On summer and evening dresses, wear straps set far apart, and, as seen here, cap sleeves on dresses and t-shirts; slashed or boat necklines all add to the illusion of broader shoulders.

### To narrow over-broad shoulders
Here, the opposite rules apply: do NOT wear slashed, boat-neck or cap-sleeved tops. Take out all shoulder pads and wear thin straps on dresses, not too wide apart. Set-in sleeves in jackets and dresses also give a more tailored, narrow, look, and a deeper neckline will always take the eye away from the shoulders!

## Bustline

### To add inches
Bulky, textured fabric will make a difference as will horizontal lines, but be careful here in case the lines add too much width. Breast pockets help, as do obviously padded and uplift bras, and if you are very small busted you can get away with extremely low necklines for that 'model' look. For summer holidays, high-waisted swimsuits also give an illusion of a larger bustline.

### To make a bustline less obvious
Plain fabrics camouflage well, and loose sleeves, such as Dolmans, also work well. Vertical or diagonal patterns on tops slim and lengthen, and now you can buy excellent minimizer bras. For summer holidays, look for wrap-over swimsuits as these are very flattering to a fuller bust.

## Midriff

### To focus attention

A wonderful way of drawing attention to a good midriff and fine waist is to wear a knotted blouse, or to wrap the waist in a wide belt, or several thin belts for a fashion statement. You can also tuck tops in tightly to bottom halves, and choose high-waisted skirts and trousers for added style. Always be careful of wearing the correct kind of clothes, however, for work.

### To lengthen

Skirts with yokes on the front—i.e. an inverted triangle shape at the front—will draw the eye down and away from the waist, as will the new hipster style trousers and skirts, but be sure that the figure is trim when choosing this style. Bulging bare tummies do NOT look attractive, are certainly not correct in a formal office, and there is 'that' time of age when this becomes a real no-no. Belts can now be found that are curved in shape and hang well on the hips, thus lengthening the midriff, and any top garment worn over skirts and trousers, or even 'bloused', give an impression of length.

## Tummies

If you have a flat tummy, lucky you, and you can do whatever you like to show it off. Do beware, though: bare midriffs, tattoos, and piercings are definitely not appropriate at work.

### TO CAMOUFLAGE LARGER TUMMIES

As before, the universal solution is to steer clear of shiny fabrics and wear matt fabric to avoid shine and take attention away. Flat-fronted skirts, especially those with stitched down pleats, help give support to tums, as do control pants available everywhere. A front zip, say on jeans, can add rather a lot of bulk to a rounded tum. Skirts/trousers with no (or small) waistbands also minimize tums as will the inevitable vertical lines!

## HIPS AND THIGHS

Here, once more, lucky you if you don't have a problem, wear tight pants and mini skirts with aplomb in your leisure time! Do be careful of over-casual dressing at work.

### TO MAKE THEM LOOK SMALLER

Guess what? Vertical lines! And, at the other end of your body, wearing shoulder pads—not too large, we're not talking Dynasty here—will make larger hips look more in proportion and will do wonders for your waist by making it appear smaller in contrast. Shoulder pads in soft foam are available at many large stores in the haberdashery departments. Do try this: you'll be surprised at the improvement when either tucked under a bra strap or stitched into the shoulder of the garment.

Dark, matt colours, and cover-ups down to knuckle length are the right length to wear, longer than that can be overpowering and swamping. Bear your height in mind. Sew down gaping side pockets on trousers and choose knee-length skirts and shorts which work proportionately better

## Big Bum?

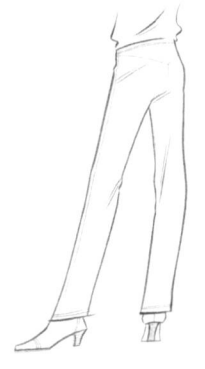

If you want to wear trousers but feel that you have an overlarge backside, the best method is to wear longer jackets and tops to cover the offending area! However, if you don't want to do this, then just make sure that the trousers you are wearing are darker in colour and have no rear pockets (especially with flaps), or are not in a thick fabric which just exaggerates the fullness of the figure. A rear V-shaped welt on the pants will lessen the impression of size, but beware of a horizontal line running across the back of the pants as this will undoubtedly exaggerate the problem.

### To flatter a small backside

In this case you can do exactly the opposite and wear tight trousers with back pockets and detailing. Colour is not an issue. However do be careful not to wear unsuitably tight pants at work.

## Calves and Ankles

If you have thicker legs than you'd like, do be careful not to make them seem even thicker. Skirts stopping across the calf can give the false impression that the part of the leg that you can't see is wider than the width of the calf which is unflattering. If you are worried about your leg shape wear skirts that stop on the knee or on the ankle, do not wear midi length except when wearing long boots. Thicker ankles are also a problem these days with so many ankle-strapped shoes around. These straps form a horizontal line across the ankle and draw attention to it, and foreshorten the leg, so try to wear a medium or high heeled court shoe, simple and plain. In a perfect world, wear a beige colour with skin-tone tights: this will lengthen and slim the leg and ankle. The alternative to this is to wear a black skirt, black tights and black court shoes for a similar effect. Wearing the same toned skirt, tights and shoes is very slimming, especially when dark coloured. A diagonal strap across the foot on a shoe works well for a slimmer look.

**FINER LEGS**

These lucky ladies with long slim legs can wear pretty much what they want and draw attention to their ankles and calves with strappy sandals. Finely proportioned shoes with thin straps make slim ankles look great. Skirt lengths can be any length you choose, bearing in mind that in an office, short skirts are not really appropriate.

If your problem is that you have legs that are a little too thin, then look to fitted and elasticated boots (to avoid sag). It can be hard to find really skinny shaped boots for thinner legs. Of course some boots now are designed to be saggy and look great worn with opaque tights in the winter. Obviously, trousers are great for camouflaging thinner legs both in winter and summer.

*Women's Issues*

## Hair

How many times have you asked your friends, family and finally your hairdresser "What shall I do with my hair?" If our hair is curly we want it straight, if our hair is straight we want it curly, if we're blonde we want to be brunette and vice versa—are we ever going to be satisfied? Our so-called 'crowning glories' seem to be the bane of our lives so here is a little advice which might help you.

### First of all, colour.

Not everyone wants to colour their hair, and in fact I didn't choose to colour my own until very recently, (maybe the grey hair was beginning to become a little dominant!), but choosing the right colour for you shouldn't be a haphazard choice. Unless you have no problem in dyeing your hair pink, blue or green, most of us would prefer to have a natural colour, but that natural colour really needs to complement our skin tones in order to make us look at our best. If your skin has pink tones choose neutral tones like ash blonde, ash brown or dark brown. Don't choose red or yellow-blonde which will be too warm for your complexion.

If your skin is olive, then stay dark. Perhaps you could add a few rich low lights in chestnut or burgundy but keep them aligned with your skin tone.

If your skin is very pale and has no freckles and no obvious pink in it, then you can wear almost any colour you choose as your skin tone won't 'fight' with your hair.

If your skin is yellow-toned or sallow, dark rich shades such as burgundy or deep auburn will work well. Do not choose colours with a yellow undertone.

Tip: Make sure, if you do dye your hair, that eyebrows and make-up are all in complementary tones.

What hairstyle should I choose for my face shape?

### Your Facial Features

First of all, what kind of face do you have, is it angular or is it soft in features?

## Soft Features

If you can clearly see that you have rounded eyes, curved eyebrows, soft cheeks, a soft nose, mouth and a rounded chin, you can be sure of having a soft-featured face. However, not everyone can be all soft featured, so take a balanced view of your face and if one set of features, e.g. eyes, eyebrows, nose and cheeks are soft and your mouth and jawline are more angular, then your predominance of soft features will decide your face-type.

This will then lead to your choice of softer hairstyles and hats, glasses and softer styled clothing. Steer clear of sharp tailoring and geometric prints, and look for softer, gentler styling.

## Angular Features

In contrast to the softer featured face, the angular face is all strong lines. Almond eyes, straight eyebrows, straight nose, angular cheeks, jawbone and straight lips. Again, the look can be softened with large eyes, for example, or more curving eyebrows. It is the predominance of one set of feature over another that will make the face angular or not. If it is strongly angular then, once again, clothing, hairstyles, glasses and hats are all angular in style and the style of the angular featured person is more geometric and sharp. This person should avoid soft curving styles as they will battle with their stronger features.

## Face Shapes

### Oval Face

This really is the most versatile of all face-shapes and you can wear any hairstyle you wish. You can grow it long and then wear it up, keep it short and sassy or choose a medium length cut. Fringes do make a style more versatile, but again it isn't necessary. However, if you cut your hair short, a fringe is normally a part of the style.

### Heart-shaped Face

This face-shape normally has a wide forehead and wide cheekbones with a pointed chin. In this case, if you have height at the top of your haircut and side partings, this will minimise any width. Styles which hang long and soft into the neck are also flattering, and flipping hair out at the level of your chin will also give the illusion of a wider jawline. It is inadvisable to have very short hair, and a short solid fringe will make your cheeks appear much fuller.

### Round Face

Feather hair around the face to minimise the roundness of your cheeks. Height on the top of your style will also lengthen your look, as will an asymmetrical style with, for example, one side tucked behind your ear and the rest of the hair falling across the forehead—this will define your face.

Short styles will just accentuate the round shape and anything that is too flat against the face will also make your face look shorter and fuller. Avoid middle partings as these just add breadth to the face.

## Square Face

Your face structure can be quite strong, so it is better to soften this look with a longer, layered style, including a light fringe. The top layers can add height, which will give the impression that the face is longer and draw it a little from its 'square' look.

A short style is too severe for you and can be seen as rather masculine. A full straight fringe will also add extra width and overpower your face.

## Rectangular Face

With a long narrow face and angular outlines you need to balance your look with width and fullness. Fringes can shorten the face but hair taken up can just exaggerate the length of the face unless a fringe is cut. For real emphasise and a style statement you can even go for straight hair in a strong bob but you need to be aiming for a definite 'look' to do this!

## Overall

Do try to keep a versatility in your choice of hairstyle so that you can change your look depending upon what your choice of clothing is going to be. It can be casual when you want to be casual and more formal when that matters more.

It is inadvisable to take a photo in to your hairdresser and ask him/her to cut/colour your hair in that style. You may have totally different hair to the model in the picture and your face-shape may just not suit that style, let alone the colour of your skin probably not being right for the colour chosen. Talk over your choices with your hairdresser and a good stylist should be able to find the right style for you, your face and your lifestyle. If you do have colour on your hair, ensure that you have it touched up regularly as obvious roots spoil a good hairstyle and ruin the image.

## Footwear

The most obvious comment is "keep shoes clean!" Nothing lets a smart outfit down more than down-at-heel shoes, so keep them polished and have them repaired before they become run down. If you buy good quality shoes you should only need 2 pairs per season. Do walk around in them in the shop before buying—hot feet from shopping can be a disaster to the right fit. I prefer to buy a half-size too large and put a shoe-sock inside.

### Court Shoes

Of all the shoe designs on the market, the court shoe is without doubt the bestseller. With a heel of 3-4 cm, the court shoe is comfortable to walk in and it complements most dress, skirt and trouser styles.

Tip: Court shoes worn with trousers look most stylish when most of the foot is covered, or matching tights are worn, so buy styles where the front of the shoe is high cut or you have tights to match if you plan to wear them with trousers. The trousers should stop approximately 1.5cm above the heel at the back and have one 'bend' on the front where they touch the shoe. Be aware of an 'ankle swinger' look and if wearing deliberately cut-off trousers, make sure you are making a definite statement and aren't wearing trousers that just look too short!

Many women wear 5-6 cm heel height for daywear. It is slightly higher than the classic court shoe, but can still be worn for everyday wear, particularly if you're in a job that allows you to drive to work and change when you get there. If not, travel in some loafers and carry your heels in your bag! However, it isn't appropriate to wear very high and sexy shoes to work.

Unless you have very slim long legs, avoid ankle straps and t-straps, as these foreshorten the leg and draw attention to thicker ankles. Straps at an angle across the foot can be the exception to this rule, as diagonal patterns in any form of clothing are slimming.

### Sling-backs

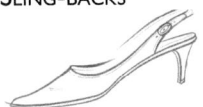

These shoes need good ankles and calves to look flattering. Make sure, if you choose to wear this style, that you have taken care of the skin on your heels, that it is well-conditioned and all dry skin near the sole removed. If not, it can look less than attractive. It is also quite often unsuitable to wear open-toed (sandal-style) shoes at work.

### Fabric Shoes

Although suede and fabric shoes can be useful, they lose colour and look old quite quickly, so beware of these for work. Do ensure that they are kept clean with a suede brush and custom cleaner.

### Shoes for chunky legs

If your legs are less than perfect, go for elegant simple shapes and avoid very high cut shoes. Make sure you look at your feet in a mirror when you try on shoes and check them from all angles. The longer the shoe the slimmer your feet and ankles will look, and a neutral colour shoe worn with neutral tights will also make the leg look longer and slimmer. Remember, avoid ankle straps as these will further thicken the look of the ankles.

### Boots

There are so many shapes and sizes to choose from in the High Street. The main point of style to remember is that it is advisable not to wear a skirt that stops short of the top of your boots leaving a small gap where the legs can be seen. Better to wear a longer skirt over the top of the boots for a more sleek, put together look, or short ankle boots as an alternative. However, be aware that for those with chunkier legs this can be less than flattering. Better to cover the legs with skirt and boots, or wear smart court shoes with a knee length skirt and, if possible, keep shoes, skirt and tights in the same dark matching colour, preferably black, for a really chic stylish effect. Some people have a problem finding boots for bigger legs. Look for elasticated gussets around the zip or stretch fabric boots.

It is a very good idea to have shoe-trees for your boots and shoes. The longer tall trees hold boots and keep them less saggy, and shoe-trees in shoes keep them crease-free and will certainly extend their lives if used regularly from new. Polish ought, ideally, to be applied when the shoes are warm from wearing because the polish is absorbed more easily.

## WARDROBE WORKOUTS (WOMEN)

Have you stood in front of your wardrobe lately and shaken your head in distress at the clutter? Is it time you took command of your wardrobe and stopped it controlling you? Find some large bin liners, take a deep breath and start the process of clearing the rack of unwanted, unworn and out of date garments. You will feel so much better for it—it truly will be a cathartic experience.

Make 4 piles:
1. Clothes that don't fit well.
2. Clothes that are the wrong colour or style for you.
3. Clothes that are more than 3 years old, and,
4. Clothes that you wear often.

First of all take out anything that doesn't fit you any more. Ask yourself honestly, "Am I ever going to fit into this?" "Do I really intend to lose the inches to get me back into it?" This is a decision for you to make, but if it is really too small (or too large for that matter) and in your honest self-questioning you know you probably won't get back to quite that size again (and nothing is more unflattering than over-tight or baggy clothes), then put it into the bin liner and start the process of de-cluttering. (Hint: sometimes, when I feel a bit big for a garment, especially a pair of jeans, I keep it and use it as a measuring device to see how my diet is going—much better than weighing myself constantly or getting out the tape measure – and how great is it when you can get back in to them comfortably?!).

Once you understand what colours and styles really suit you, you'll be able to see at a glance what colours and styles of garments should be removed and unceremoniously dumped! Be bold, clear them out; if anything is of particular value or sentimental value, then hang it up with a plastic cover and put it somewhere—the attic for example—where, if you still don't wear it for a couple of years, you really know that it is a white elephant (or an heirloom). Don't forget the principle of cost per wear—divide the number of times you have worn something into the original price paid and see how much it has cost you each time you have worn it! An outfit bought for a special occasion may have cost hundreds of pounds, and you've worn it once? If you wear it 10 times it will have cost 1/10$^{th}$ of the purchase price each time you wore it. Much better value for money—so buy with that in mind every time—you need your clothes to be versatile.

Look at the styles and older clothes that are left hanging in the wardrobe. Are they saying "this person is modern and trendy, or classic or contemporary?" Whatever they say, is it what you want to be? Once again, be strong and throw out anything that really doesn't suit how you want to be perceived. Have a vision of what you want to achieve in your personal brand packaging.

The fourth pile is going to be all the clothes that you wear most of the time. It won't be a big pile. Do you know we wear 20% of our clothes 80% of the time? Look at them and see why you wear them. They fit well? They are in a colour and style that suits you? They are appropriate to your life-style? You can wear them often to all sorts of occasions? Let me tell you about the Rule of Three. When you go shopping and you find a really wonderful garment that you really really want. Stop! Stand back, look at it and ask yourself three questions;

- Can I wear this garment to three occasions?
- Can I wear it through three seasons?
- Can I wear it with three other things in my wardrobe?

If you can't answer 'yes' to all of these questions PUT IT BACK! – especially if you can't afford to buy all the other things to go with it, whether it be shoes, trousers, coats or skirts.

So now you have cleared out all unworn items, now stand back and re-organise what is left. Ladies, split suits and hang skirts and trousers separately from jackets. Don't believe that old wives' tale that says you will wear out one garment before another—we don't keep things or wear them enough to do that! By splitting up your suits you will find that other garments go with them to make whole new outfits. For example, a red suit can often mix well with a black suit. This way you can begin to build your capsule wardrobe, a mix-and-match wardrobe that will work together and give you really good value for money. You will also begin to see clearly what other garments you need to buy that will make it work even better for you. If you have a favourite garment that fits really well but isn't the best colour for you, wear a complementary shirt/blouse/top/scarf/necklace underneath or over it in your best colour to bring the colour back to your cheeks. What is ideal is to have your garments hanging in categories together, i.e. blouses, trousers, jackets etc. where you can see all the different variations you have.

If you feel you can't ditch all the unsuitable garments that you have recognised, put them back for now, but promise yourself to change them as soon as you can. In future, make sure you can see ALL your clothes. Garments you can't see will probably be forgotten! A six-monthly regular clear out is a really good idea.

So there you are. You are now the proud owner of a well-matched, slimmed down and versatile wardrobe. Make a list of those garments, shoes and accessories that need to be purchased to complete the working collection and plan your buying trips over the coming months. If you like to budget, do remember your life-style needs and look at how you spend your time. How much of your working day is spent at the office, how much in leisure activities, how much in sport and how much socialising? Divide your expenditure accordingly: if you spend more time working than anything else then your wardrobe should reflect that, especially if you work in a 'suited and booted' environment.

## **FIT AND CARE OF CLOTHING**

### **FIT**

The trouble with shopping is finding the size that fits you. Quite frequently, the difference in sizing can make a person who is a normal size 14, find themselves buying, to their distress, a size 16. Don't let this anomaly get to you! Different manufacturers from different countries have different pattern sizes and it isn't you that has changed, but the designer you are buying from. Ignore the size label if you can and go with a good fit first and foremost.

An elegantly comfortable fit is what you should be aiming for. Nothing looks worse than clinging clothes that show up underwear bulges and over-large garments that cover up a pretty figure (teenage fads excepted!).

Do make sure that seams are not stretched: for example, there should be an ease of at least ½"(1.5cm) on either side of a skirt and it should hang straight without folding across the hips and stomach. Pockets shouldn't gape, and in fact I often sew down my side pockets on trousers as gaping trouser pockets can add width to hips. There shouldn't be too tight a fit across the bottom, and trousers and skirts should fall well straight from the buttocks, not cling (unless the intention is for a figure-hugging look). Allow plenty of 'give' on shoulder seams, too: usually the seams extend 1 – 1½" (2+cm) beyond the shoulder. If necessary, buy a larger size (yes, you can ignore the label!) and have it taken in, rather than buying a size too small.

Look at the construction of the items you buy. An expensive garment may not be as well made as you think. These following rules apply to both men and women's garments.

- Patterns should match at seams, but in poorly manufactured garments often don't.
- Seams should not be wrinkled or pulled and should have a good finish on the edges.
- Hems should hang straight and unwrinkled.
- Pockets should fit well, be well-finished and lie flat on the garment.

- Check for loose threads, especially on button-holes and buttons.
- Make sure any linings are not stretched or over-large.
- Lapels should lie flat.

## Care of Clothing

Check the care label so that the garment will perform the working task you require and not require constant dry cleaning, which is harsh and expensive. Also look for garments that allow you to machine-wash rather than hand-wash, which can be time consuming.

On the question of dry cleaning—try to avoid it as much as possible. The use of chemicals on the fabrics can spoil the finish and weaken the structure of the fabric, especially in men's suiting. If at all possible, find a shop that will sponge and steam rather than chemically clean. It is a great idea to have a trouser press which can add years to your trousers' lives, and you always look well groomed.

Hang delicate garments on padded hangers, and suits and trousers on wooden hangers. Please don't use wire hangers: they make unsightly points in shoulders and creases on trousers. Skirts should be hung from the waistband on clipped hangers: don't use the loops that are stitched in because these cause the skirt to sag. Gentlemen, trousers should be hung upside down from gripping hangers or folded over padded bar hangers. Hang garments outside the wardrobe overnight to let the air circulate, and if possible, rotate suits—the perfect number of suits to have is 5, one for each working day. (Tip: I was told once by a very experienced tailor that you should beware of wearing a navy suit and sitting in a leather chair because blue suiting will quickly develop a shine that is impossible to remove!).

Sometimes when travelling you unpack to find a garment rather creased despite all your best attempts to pack it neatly. Hang it in the hotel bathroom and fill the tub with hot water to steam the creases out. A good purchase is a sticky roller which is great for removing fluff and hairs and general day to day dust. Sticky tape wrapped around the hand, sticky-side out, can work as well.

You will also find in this book a section on emergency grooming kits. Do make sure that you always have at hand a small needle and thread set to fix loose buttons and hems.

## SKINCARE, COSMETICS AND THEIR APPLICATION

No matter what your age, over application of make-up is very distracting and, rather than enhancing your look, can work in quite the opposite manner. A well-made up face should look natural and let your inner beauty shine through.

My advice is that 'less is more': avoid, especially in the business arena, bright blues, neon and strong make-up colours. An over-tanned look, whether real or cosmetically applied, can look leathery and, of course, if real can do serious damage to your skin.

Conversely, a face that is bare of make-up can lead to concerns that the individual is lacking in self-esteem. (Strangely this also applies to ladies who wear too much!). The basic fact of life is that women who wear at least a touch of make-up have a 20-30% better chance of promotion in the workplace. A Mamermesh-Biddle (US) study revealed that attractive people have higher incomes in general, and as, in our society, make-up is regarded as adding a finishing touch to a woman's image, then if tastefully applied it follows that appropriate cosmetics make a woman more attractive.

Good skincare is essential for a healthy look. Start with a scrupulously clean face that is well moisturised, and, if you can manage it, a regular visit to a beautician for a facial will keep your skin plumped up and looking lovely. Spots and patchy skin can shift attention from your eyes and mouth and become distracting. Exfoliation is a great way to keep your skin healthy and a once-a-week mild exfoliant should be enough. A face mask, too, is a good idea from time to time. It lifts impurities out and also gives you a chance to take it easy for ten minutes! Personally I feel that foundation is not necessary unless you have blemishes such as small thread veins which need to be covered up. A good tinted moisturizer is often enough to give a healthy glow to most skins, and especially to older skins where foundation can lay in lines in the face and give an older impression.

All daytime make-up should be applied in daylight or, if you rise too early for that, invest in a daylight bulb which will give the kind of light that you need. If you make up under electric light you will find on emerging into the daylight that you have an over-applied look. Electric light is fine if you are making up for an evening out.

A slight, well-blended, slick of blusher high on each cheek-bone heightens the healthy look. Some women prefer a matt look, in which case a touch over with a powder—for example, Boots No 7 Translucent Compact—is sufficient. If you have dark shadows or the occasional blemish, Yves St. Laurent's concealer wand Touche Eclat is a wonderful product with light reflecting properties and lifts the dark shadows with just a fine application.

Eyebrows need to be well groomed and carefully shaped, and their fine definition makes the face complete. Tidy up stray hairs but the days of thinning them out into a narrow arch are, thank goodness, over. If they are pale do consider having them gently tinted to a deeper tone, but avoid strong colours. If hair is light the eyebrows should be close matched. Eyebrows should start immediately above the inside corner of the eye. To find the correct side point of the eyebrow, take a pencil or long make-up brush and angle it from the corner of your nostril to the outside point of your eye and roll it on up. Where the pencil crosses the brow-bone is where the eyebrow should finish, this gives a balanced and well defined line.

Daytime eye-shadows should be in soft browns, greys, plums, rose and taupe depending upon your own particular colouring. If you are blonde, use brown mascara and, if a brunette, a black or dark chocolate brown one. Of course, tinting can also apply to eyelashes, too, if they are very pale, which is especially effective when going on holiday. 'Blend, blend, blend' is my mantra when applying any make-up!

Do make sure that you have good quality eye make-up brushes and keep them regularly cleaned. You will find that shorter-haired brushes are excellent for shadow coverage and blending, and a wedge-shaped brush particularly good for adding gentle colour to your eyebrows. I recommend Estee Lauder's block-powder eyebrow colours in various shades for a natural in-filler for eyebrows: use it sparingly with a wedge-shaped eyebrow brush for a natural look.

Quality makeup brushes are just as important as makeup itself. Applicators included with most makeup kits are simply not right for the job. Poor quality blush brushes are usually too small and too coarse to enable you to apply makeup properly. This is why you see some women with unattractive strips of blusher that look so unblended on the skin.

I cannot emphasize enough the value of good quality makeup tools. It is not an area to skimp on. When properly cared for, good brushes can last many years. You will get a more natural and longer lasting look, and have greater control of your makeup technique.

If you have a limited budget, start with just three or four basic brushes such as blush, eyeliner, eyebrow and shadow. Then add on from there.

Lipsticks.
Again, less is more, and there are some lovely, lightly textured and glossy lipsticks that just give a hint of colour rather than a greasy slick – beware of lipstick on teeth! You can stop this happening by simply sucking on your forefinger after applying the lipstick!

Hands and Nails.
Good nail and hand care is essential. Nothing is more off-putting than bitten and poorly maintained nails. Use a rich handcream and, if at all possible, a regular manicure is a wonderful and relaxing thing as well as keeping your nails in great condition. However, home manicures are easy to do. Keep an emery board in your bag, briefcase or desk drawer for emergency use. It is better to see bare, clean and healthy nails than chipped varnish which looks careless and slovenly. A clear coat of varnish adds shine and is often easier to maintain, too.

Teeth and Breath.
Bad breath can often stem from badly-maintained teeth. Bad breath was a high scorer in recent research on the biggest turn-offs when socialising and in business.

Body Odour.
There are no excuses for not showering daily and wearing a clean shirt or top every day. It is old sweat coming into contact with body heat that causes the problem. Natural fibres do help the body breathe more easily, but ladies, this issue does normally apply more to men than to us!

**CASUAL DISASTERS FOR WOMEN**

Maybe a little extreme, but I hope you get the picture!
Not quite right for the office!

This section is really aimed at those of you who work in a formal 'suited' environment, and who sometimes have a dress-down day. Creative and relaxed environments may accept some of the following, but even those companies who have a dress-down environment may need some form of 'code' that states what can and can't be worn to keep the 'business' environment controlled. It is harder for women to choose appropriate casual clothing for work as there is so much more choice than there is for men, but the following pointers should help:

## WHAT TO AVOID

- Denim generally is not professional in offices except in a creative environment
- T-shirts with logos
- T-shirts with logos worn under white shirts
- Shorts, unless you happen to work in a hot climate where they are generally accepted, in which case they should be tailored
- Sleeveless tops
- Visible tattoos
- Any kind of sportswear e.g. trainers, track suits, track bottoms, white socks
- Cowboy boots
- Sandals, flip flops
- Piercings of any sort
- A careless attitude to grooming—no make-up or too much!
- Chipped nail varnish (better to wear none).
- Poor hair care.
- Un-ironed clothing
- Too much personal jewellery
- Toting your possessions in carrier bags
- Strappy or strapless tops
- Visible underwear—particularly 'strings' worn with the new fashion for hipster trousers
- Leggings—yes they still appear!
- Bare legs are not business-like
- Holes and runs in stockings/tights
- Open-toed and strappy heeled shoes

### Business Casual Is:

- Immaculate grooming at all times no matter what the dress code is.
- Clothes which are laundered and pressed, in good repair and contemporary in style.
- Smedley cotton, cotton and fine knitted shirts and sweaters.
- Casual, unstructured suits and trouser suits.
- Colourful separates that mix and match well.
- Suede and leather jackets, as long as they are in good condition.
- Good quality round, scooped or v-necked tee-shirts without logos can look good under jackets.
- Comfortable but smart casual shoes: toes should still be covered.
- Leather belts (to match) of any sort.
- Quality accessories and jewellery—not too much!

### Smart Business Wear

Left: For the straight figure and angular face

Right: For the curved figure and soft face.

## More Smart Business Wear

Left: for the tapered figure (smart casual) and

Right: for the fuller figure, this look would also modify well for the evening.

*Women's Issues*

## A Basic Smart Business Wardrobe For Women

This is just an idea of what you could buy to start a basic wardrobe and then, over the years, add to it to improve and keep it up to date. Try to buy classic/contemporary styles that won't date so that the wardrobe lasts well, and you are delivering great cost per wear!

- SUITS – Two that interchange: One solid and one patterned or....
- One SOLID SUIT + one patterned jacket + one co-ordinating skirt or trousers
- BLOUSES/TOPS – 5/6 fine knits, blouses or shirts
- One long-sleeved simple DRESS that can be elegantly accessorised
- One TRENCH or OVERCOAT in your best neutral shade
- One pair black COURT SHOES + one pair of neutral courts (beige, tan, taupe)
- Don't forget good quality belts, handbags and a portfolio/briefcase that reflects your personality and style. Square, hard topped briefcases are now rather dated. Softer leather versions not dissimilar to small knapsacks and laptop bags are becoming very popular now.

**Notes**

TO IMPROVE AND MOVE ON, I WILL ...

DATE:_____

# Chapter 5

*"Adults are more likely to act their way into a new way of thinking than to think their way into a new way of acting"* Richard Pascale

## Men's Issues

### Style Matters

In these days of personal branding and the growing importance of visibility at work, when a job is not for life any more, it is important to know how to make the best of yourself, both in your personal grooming and in the clothes you choose to wear to make the best possible impact on your peers, your bosses and your clients.

There has been enormous growth in the men's personal grooming industry, and there is now a huge range of products available over the counter. It is as commonplace for men to take care of their skin and hair, without feeling uncomfortable about it, as their wives/girlfriends have always done. Men-only spas are opening all over the country and the rise in plastic surgery and botox injections for men is exponential. Men have realised that taking care of their appearance in our 21$^{st}$ Century environment is necessary and pays dividends in terms of self-assurance and self-promotion.

I plan to lay in front of you a few style guidelines that you can follow to help you choose clothes. By working with the figure you have and to the style that you prefer, these will suit you well. You will also see how to define your face type so that you will know how to choose glasses, hairstyles and necklines, including those shirts for work that are now available in so many collar-shapes that it is confusing to know which to choose. Then I will put together some ideas for you to plan a wardrobe that will suit your lifestyle and budget.

## FIGURE ANALYSIS

There are basically 3 male figure types, with naturally loads of individual proportional differences, but it is a simple matter to see where you fit in.

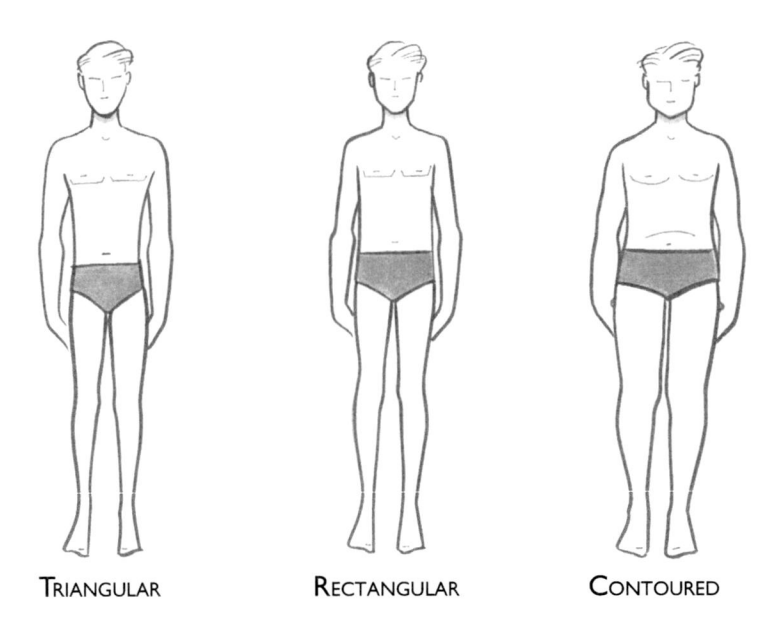

| TRIANGULAR | RECTANGULAR | CONTOURED |

### MR TRIANGULAR

This figure type is broad shouldered, the shoulders being much broader than the waist which appears small and with narrow hips. This gives a triangular look to the body and you can be a tall or smaller version of this shape. You do not have to be a muscle man to be triangular, although some men may become this shape after a lot of heavy work or exercise.

### MR RECTANGULAR

The majority of men that I have met during my workshops and personal consultations seem to fit this shape. It is basically a straight body shape, shoulders, chest, waist and hips being pretty much the same size and forming the rectangular shape. It is a good shape to be so long as you are relatively slim and fit as you will be able to wear a large selection of clothes. Again you can be any height but still be rectangular in shape.

### MR CONTOURED

This is for the 'fuller' chap. Sloping shoulders, a full 'corporation' or just a rounded tum, and a wide ribcage. You may well have put on weight having once been rectangular or triangular, but this is not necessarily the case: it can be just a more rounded look to the body. 'Stocky' or 'thickset' can be used to describe this shape.

It is important to keep your own body shape clearly in mind, as if you try to wear clothes that would be designed for a different shape, it will never look as good on you as you would like. Imagine trying to fit a rectangle into a triangle, or a triangle into a contoured shape and you can see that it could look ridiculous. Buy clothes that suit your body shape: the fit will be excellent and you will feel at ease.

## Issues of Scale and Personal Accessories

'Scale' is a much neglected area and it is surprisingly important. If you are a 'vertically challenged' man, probably under 5'6" with fine bones, fine features and small hands and feet, a huge chronometer on your wrist will make you look even smaller. Carrying a large briefcase will do exactly the same: surrounding yourself with large objects will exaggerate your smaller size and shape. However, bearing your stature in mind you can wear neater and less heavy watches, and carry finer bags and look so much more in proportion.

The other side of this issue is the large man who wears over-small pieces, you can go for large fountain pens, larger (but not too flashy, please) cufflinks, bold watches and larger bags. All these will form an image of a smaller person as, once again, you are in proportion.

On the topic of personal accessories, don't overdo it. When I am asked how much accessorising a person should do, I always say "never more than 10 pieces!" A man, especially in business, should wear a wedding band (if applicable!) or signet ring, cufflinks and a good watch (not a swatch type watch). He should have quality 'extras' such as a good fountain pen (not a chewed biro), and a quality briefcase—the style is becoming softer and usually has a shoulder strap—we are getting away from the square, valise-style briefcase. Pierced ears should be saved for social life, never in the office.

# SCALE

Overlarge accessories on a small frame – just make you look smaller!

# SCALE

Too small accessories, e.g. belts, watches, folders, will make you look larger!

When buying your clothing, you will obviously have to know where you intend to wear it. Are you buying for your social life or for work? If you are in an office environment where the suit is the accepted form of wear, then think carefully about your purchases. A suit is one of the most expensive things you will ever have in your wardrobe, so decide on the colour, pattern, fabric weight and style you want. Settle on the price you are prepared to pay and know your size. This is not a purchase to be made in 5 minutes. Please do good research and go out with time to spare; don't rush the purchase of a suit as it will be an expensive mistake if anything is wrong with it.

Not everyone has to wear a suit to work: quite often casual clothing that is smart can be worn at work and socially, so these items of clothes are probably worn more frequently. Look for quality when shopping—quality fabric and construction will last longer than cheaper alternatives. A well-constructed and expensive jacket will repay the wearer many times over in terms of the amount it is worn and its 'cost per wear' value.

'Cost per wear?' Imagine that you buy a suit for £350.00 and you wear it 3 times a week for say 48 weeks: it costs you approximately £2.40 each time you wear it. Wear it 3 times a week for 2 years and the price has come down to £1.20 per wear, and that's really good value for money. Wear it just a couple of times because you're not very keen on it for some reason and it has cost you £175.00 each time out. Choose wisely!

Quality clothes should last longer especially if you take good care of them. Don't dry-clean them too often because it will eventually stretch the fibres within the fabric: sponge them instead or have them steamed. Hang them up at night outside the wardrobe to air, and preferably have a trouser press for the trousers. It is also a good idea, if possible, to have an extra pair of trousers for each suit you have.

## PROPORTIONAL ISSUES IN MENS' WEAR.

### MR. TRIANGULAR
Because of your broad shoulders, you don't need much padding in your jackets—in fact, too much can look comical and rather dated. However, you can take a wide lapel, and even super-wide if you have an angular face as well. (see later). Double-breasted suits will look great on you, and you

can also wear well-tailored single breasted jackets too—avoid the 'boxy' look. You can go for strong geometric shapes and steer clear of soft shapes and curves. Keep the look 'strong'. Because you have a defined waist then do choose belts and blouson jackets to exaggerate your figure and when it comes to trousers you can wear double pleats, slim fitted trousers and tuck in tops if you want to, I think the tucked-in look is now a little dated in casual wear, but if tops are hanging over your trousers, your slim figure is being covered up - your choice!

### Mr Rectangle

You can choose to wear strong shoulder pads or not as you desire. Sharply notched lapels or more rounded ones are your choice too. You can also choose to wear angular shapes or more soft ones according to your taste e.g. jacket hemlines. Trousers are better with single pleats coming from the waistline, not too bulky, and a regular fit, straight-legged trouser is your recommended style. Belts can be worn to bring attention to trim waists, but beware if you have any excess weight, tucked in <u>casual</u> tops only look good on you where there is no 'bulge' underneath (or over!).

### Mr Contoured

Be careful not to wear too much padding in your jacket shoulders as you are already a good size and don't need improvement in that area. If your shoulders do slope then a good tailor will tailor your suit to remedy that and give you, with your curved figure, the right amount of width to flatter you and, despite the commonly-held belief that double-breasted jackets look good on a larger male figure, DON'T BELIEVE THEM!! Quite simply, a double-breasted jacket which has buttons across the front, leads the eyes to look from right to left following the invisible horizontal line formed by the button line, and makes the wearer seem much larger. A well-tailored and curved single-breasted jacket is more flattering.

Trousers should be flat-fronted: any pleats in them will exaggerate a tummy, and they should be relaxed in fit and straight-legged. Belts should always be worn if the trousers have belt-loops, but sometimes a bright belt buckle can draw the eye down to a wider than perfect waistline: in this case, braces might be better, but these should be on trousers specifically

*Men's Issues*

made for braces. The alternative is to use belts that have a leather-covered buckle or matt metal with no shine.

Casual tops should be worn outside trousers and if you choose vertical lines (such as a pinstripe in suits) rather than horizontal lines, you can achieve a slimmer effect. Do avoid large horizontal stripes in patterns and, if you are going to a formal occasion which requires a dinner jacket, discard the cummerbund for a more slimming waistcoat with diagonally pointed bottom edges (not straight) to avoid the 'ring around the barrel' problem!

## Individual style problems

### Long Necks

Wear roll collars and higher fitting shirt collars in business. Wear casual (e.g. Smedley cotton polos) buttoned up at the neck: an open collar can make the neck look even longer. Also avoid V-necks worn alone, very long pointed collars and narrow ties.

Yes    No

### Short or wide necks

In this case you can wear <u>open</u> shirts and V-necks to lengthen a neck, and find shirt collars that are cut lower. A beard will definitely make you look as though you have no neck at all! Avoid polo-necks, and contrasting collars that draw attention to the neck.

Yes    No

## Broad shoulders

Vertical and horizontal patterns and shapes are best for over-broad shoulders, so V-necks and finely knitted, vertical, cable-patterned sweaters look good. Avoid a lot of shoulder padding: strong horizontal detail across the shoulders or chest will add emphasis to a wide area. Of course, if that is what you want, go for it!

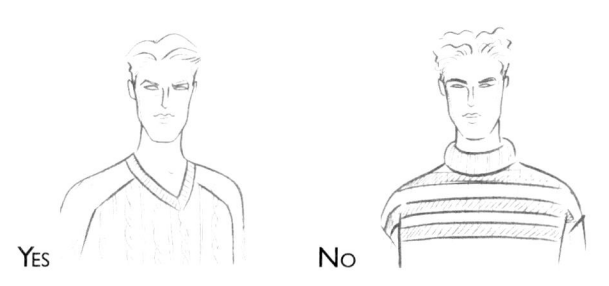

Yes        No

## Narrow shoulders

Here you can go for the shoulder pads! In contrast to the broad-shouldered, wear horizontal patterns, and bulkier sweaters. Broad checks on jackets will also add width. Avoid V-necks which will make you look narrower, as will vertical stripes.

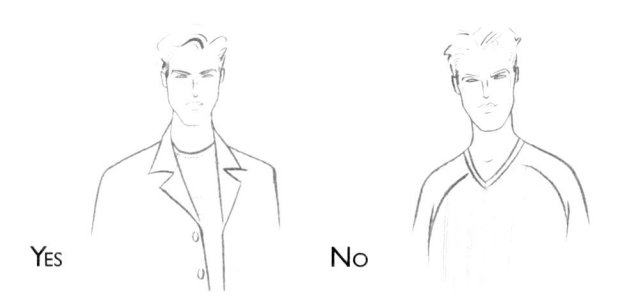

Yes        No

## Over-long legs

If you form a horizontal line across your trousers with a turn-up it will shorten the leg substantially. You can also wear longer-length jackets to disguise your leg length, but beware too-long jacket sleeves drowning you. A contrasting colour, e.g. dark blue jacket and paler trousers, will perform the function of cutting you in colour blocks (more horizontal lines) and shorten the length of legs and body. Horizontal lines on jackets will also widen and shorten the body. Pleats at the waist in trousers will also add width and take away from that 'long' look.

**OVER-LONG LEGS**

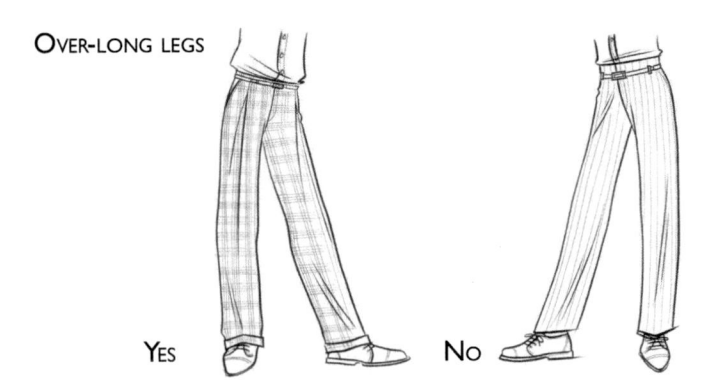

Yes    No

**TOO SHORT LEGS**
Avoid turn-ups as these will shorten the leg even further, and wide-leg trousers will also foreshorten you. Buckled over-long trousers draw the eye down and accentuate the short leg. Pleats on the waistband make bulk and not length. Go for vertical patterns in the trousers and jackets and make sure that your jackets are in proportion, i.e. not too long. Single-breasted jackets will make you look taller and wearing the same tone throughout, e.g. charcoal jacket and dark grey or black trousers will lengthen your look. Avoid jackets, or tops in a different tone to the trousers as these will cut you up in horizontal lines and make you look shorter.

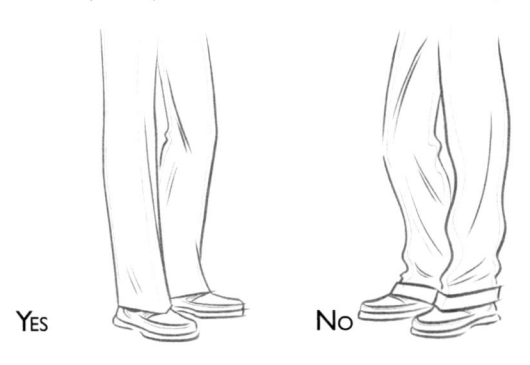

Yes    No

**A PROBLEM WITH THE 'CORPORATION'?**
Gentlemen with a bit of a tum need to choose unclingy and loose tops, The 'ease' of fit is everything as tight clothes which form bulky rings around the body will really exacerbate the problem. Don't let a tummy hang over the trousers but buy trousers that fit across it—if possible, a little above it—and wear braces to keep them up if necessary. Choose wide leg trousers and always go for the slimming vertical lines which we have

discussed before. Quite often a waistcoat with a jacket can do wonders to hide a tummy, and single-breasted jackets are much preferable to double-breasted ones. You can certainly wear a wide and interesting tie, but make sure it doesn't stop short of your trousers. Be honest with yourself and if you are growing larger, buy larger sizes. Spreading buttons on shirts, too-tight jackets and folded-over waists on tight trousers can never make a good impression.

Yes        No

## Big Bum?

Dark colours on trousers are preferable to light shades and if possible avoid jeans with large detail on the back pockets and yoke. Avoid shine, so shiny modern track-suit pants, unless covered with a long jacket, are OUT. Large patterns on trousers, such as a loud check are not a good idea. Cover up with long tops and shirts coming down to knuckle length, and probably best to avoid tucking things in when dressing casually.

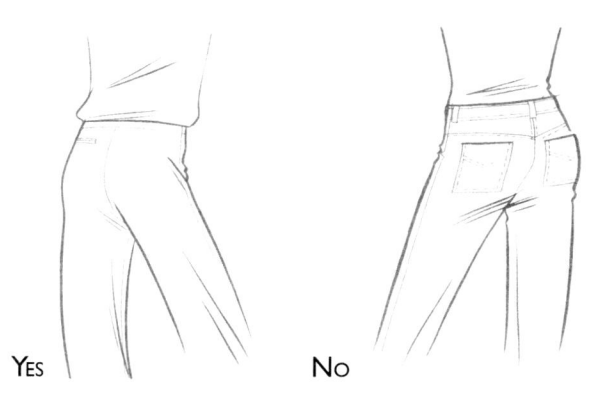

Yes        No

## Have You Considered Your 'Look' Recently?

To look powerful and well dressed, a businessman should wear clothes indicating that:

- They are complementary to his physique and colouring.
- They are contemporary without being trendy.
- They fit well. (This is very important: poorly fitted clothes—even if they are expensive—will not achieve the desired effect and you can end up looking shabby.)
- They reflect the wearer's personality—the idea of a great Personal Brand is to be consistently truthful about who you are.
- They are appropriate for his profession, his peers and his clients.
- They are in good repair and spotlessly clean.

A dinosaur approach to your appearance leads to a perception of a dinosaur mind. In the fast-moving 21st Century, it is vital to keep other people's perception of you as modern, forward thinking, dynamic and professional. Ask yourself some of the following questions and see where you fit in terms of your personal appearance.

- Have you seriously thought about your personal image at work lately, or do you automatically dress in the same clothes you've been wearing for the past few years?
- This said, do you consider fashion trends? Suits and jackets may well be similar from year to year, but shirts and ties have a distinctly different look now from, say, 5 years ago. If you work in a dress down environment, there is an even bigger change in the fashions worn at the office. Why not try some window shopping to get an idea of what's around at the moment?
- Do you have a full-length mirror at home? It is amazing how many people dress in the dark before work or look at their image in a bathroom mirror. How can you see what impression you are making if you don't take a good long look at the entire image from head to shoes?
- Talking about shoes, how are yours? Do you have pairs of shoes for work that you have been wearing for more than 3 years? Are your shoes in good repair and clean? Do your socks match your shoes? Do you match your shoes to your belt (or vice versa)?

- Do you have tattoos or piercings that are on show at work? If possible these should be covered up in a formal office setting.
- Is your personal grooming and hygiene immaculate? Do you visit the hairdresser regularly (at least once every two months)?
- Do you have an emergency repair kit in the office to fix lost buttons, etc?

## What Do You Need to Complete a Good Business Wardrobe?

This section will deal mainly with those of you who work in a formal booted and suited environment.

Of course not everyone does this and there will be a section on smart casual dressing, but for the moment, let's concentrate on those of you who have to dress more formally. What you need to do is ensure that you are getting good value out of your wardrobe, that your investment in suits lasts as long as possible and you get good cost-per-wear value out of them.

In an ideal world you should have 5 suits in your wardrobe which you can rotate on a daily basis through the week. This will help them last longer and you will get more value from them. I also recommend that you buy a spare pair of trousers with each suit to extend its life. It is a good idea to hang the suits outside the wardrobe each evening to air and breathe and, if you are travelling, try hanging the suit over your hotel bath and turning on the hot taps in the tub for a while to give it a chance to de-wrinkle in the steam and freshen up.

I recommend that you choose 4 dark suits in charcoals, navy blues and even black (for very dark haired and 'deep' individuals). It is a good idea to buy a lighter suit in a paler grey or a mid-toned blue for the less formal occasions or when you want to be less formal and more amenable—the psychological value of wearing a paler suit when wanting to be more approachable has been proved!

Choose a dozen long-sleeved shirts, preferably with a double cuff and discreet cufflinks. A double (or French) cuff is more stylish and sophisticated. Choose varying colours and patterns but do take care to select colours that really make you look well and vital—see the colour pages of this book to help you here.

Pick approximately 15 ties. When buying shirts it is a good idea to buy the ties at the same time. Lay, say, three shirts out and find a tie (the shop assistant should be able to help you here) that goes with all the shirts, and then repeat the exercise with the next three etc. This way you should be able to have a really good-mix-and-match set of ties and shirts. Again, choose ties that complement your own specific colour type.

You should have a couple of pairs of good quality lace-up brogues or toe-cap Blucher, and maybe a black slip-on for a more relaxed look—there is more detail under 'Footwear and Belts'. Do remember that socks go with shoes NOT with trousers.

Talking about socks—specifically for the office, buy a dozen or so identical pairs of natural fibre black socks, longer length, i.e. at least mid calf, then you should never have to search for matching pairs again. You know how it is, dark winter morning, trying to get dressed in the dark so as not to upset your partner, fishing around in a drawer for a matching pair. Put that all behind you! Why longer length? The half-inch of hairy ankle that shows between trouser bottoms and socks when you cross your legs is probably the most unsexy thing around—get longer socks, chaps!

**MIND THE GAP!**

## FOOTWEAR AND BELTS

The most obvious comment is "keep them clean!" Nothing lets a smart outfit down more than down-at-heel shoes, so keep them polished and repaired before they become run down.

The plain toecap Oxford lace-up is the basic shoe style for smart—though not strictly formal—office wear; an alternative to this is the Wing-tip Brogue, quite often made in suede.

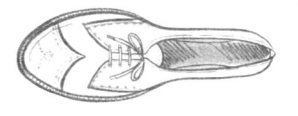

This has stitching and pinking on it, as it originated in Ireland and the Scottish Highlands. (The imitation punchings that decorate today's brogues once were actual holes or slashings made to let water drain out. Not really necessary now!)

The Blucher, named after one of Napoleon's more formidable opponents, Prussian General Gebhard Leberecht von Blucher, is a less fancy style of lace-up, still with a stitched toecap, but less formal than the Oxford.

On an equal footing with the Oxford is the Dress Slip-On, which looks good with smart office suits

Although it may not be a common term, the Monk style of low-fitting shoe, strapped across the instep and fastening through a saddle buckle on the shoe's outside, always looks elegant and goes with a diverse range of trousers.

Slip-on Moccasins can look too casual and soon become loose. It is important to make sure that these do not become too shabby to go with a smart suit. Chukka boots are not suitable for office wear, although they are great with moleskins, flannels or cords for smart dress-down occasions.

In the early 70's, Wall Street Investment bankers took to corporate chalk stripes, Turnbull & Asser spread collars, and Gucci slip-ons. Over 30 years later Gucci's buckled shoes still have style mileage to spare.

*Men's Issues*

Make sure all your smart shoes have wooden shoe-trees to keep them in shape, and if possible polish your shoes while still warm from wearing—the polish sinks in better!

## Belts

If your trousers have belt loops, please wear a belt: the trousers look unfinished and the look is sloppy without the belt for which they were designed.

Whatever style you choose make sure that your belt is the same colour as your shoes, and fastens so that the end of the belt finishes between the first and second belt loop! No less, no more. In other words, buy the right size for you.

Shiny belt buckles can draw attention to a large stomach, so if you have a 'corporation' try to find buckles that are wrapped in the same leather as the belt itself.

If you like to wear braces (or as they are known in the US – suspenders), if possible wear specially designed trousers as they are cut to be worn with braces and hang better than normal trousers worn with braces.

## Overview of a Basic Smart Business Wardrobe For Men

This is the beginning of a business wardrobe which you can develop and maintain over the years at minimum expense. Do try to buy styles that suit your figure shape and proportions and will not become outdated too quickly, so avoid 'faddy' styling and go for classic and contemporary looks.

- SUITS – minimum 2 –3 preferably 5, one for each day of the week
- 1st and 2nd SUITS in solid charcoal and solid navy.
- 3rd SUIT can be subtly patterned and/or lighter depending upon your business.
- SHIRTS – minimum 6 - 12, at least one in white or off-white, remainder in pale blue, striped or pale shades, again, dependent upon what colours really suit you best.

- SHOES –minimum 2 pairs – 1 pair with a plain toe, black and lace-ups, plus 1 pr of black or oxblood lace-up brogues. Socks to match shoes.
- BELTS to match shoes – and always wear a belt where your trousers have belt-loops. The belt should fit you properly – i.e. finish after buckling up between the first and second belt loop.
- TRENCH or OVERCOAT in neutral, navy, charcoal or black.
- TIES – minimum of 6, in silk NOT polyester, in flattering shades and appropriate patterns avoiding loud designs.

Plus good quality personal business cases and accessories,.

## Hair Today – Gone Tomorrow

- Go easy on it if your hair is thinning! When towel drying your hair don't rub your head too hard. Keep a hat on in an open car! Be kind to your hair! - don't stress it – love it!
- Massage your scalp very gently when you wash your hair –this stimulates blood supply to the follicles, and encourages growth.
- Use essential oils to feed the roots and try recommended products from specialist suppliers to slow down hair loss.
- Use products to volumise and thicken the hair – there are a lot of them out there on the market.

If it really becomes thin, go on, cut it off! It looks really great with a No. 3 cut – Phil Collins has no hair and has a huge fan club, please don't comb over!

Men's Issues

## Male Facial Features

It is a surprising fact that the shape of your face can be used to define the shape of your clothes and the patterns you wear. A face that has mainly angular lines lends itself to clothing that has angular lines and angular patterns e.g. geometric stripes, checks and diagonals. A softer, more contoured face is flattered by softer lines and patterns.

Here are some ideas to try:

### Angular Face

This face has straight lines on it, strong straight eyebrows, almond eyes, defined nose, chiselled cheeks and chin and a straight mouth

To choose the most flattering clothes that will define your image in a clear and distinct manner, choose from the following:

### Collars
Standard Collar, Tab Collar, Button Down Collar and also look at the proportional collar shapes, described later, dependent upon your particular needs (e.g. long, thin, short neck etc.)

### Patterns (Ties and Shirts)
Look for plain fabric, strong stripes, checks and any geometric shapes such as diamonds, birds-eye spots and zig-zags.

### Suit fabrics
Plain fabrics, pinstripes, chalk stripes, checks.

### Lapels
Sharp cut lapels such as notched and peaked; Mandarin collars suit well for evening wear jackets or casual shirts.

### Necklines
Again, dependent upon your other proportional issues (nothing is ever cast in stone!), angular features suit V-necks, Turtle-necks, zip-up tops, and polo shirts.

## SOFTER FACE

Sharp lines and patterns will conflict with your softer face, so think about complementary shapes and lines.

### Collars

A standard collar, a spread collar (if your face is not too round), and a rounded collar. This isn't always possible in really formal business wear, so compensate by choosing softer patterns on your tie and a less strong suit style. Remember that if you wear a spread collar you will require a larger knot in your tie.

### Patterns (Ties and Shirts)
Plain fabric, softer, less defined stripes and checks and soft self-patterns in the fabric such as polka dots.

### Lapels
Soft lapels and standard peaked lapels are the best style for the softer contours of your face. You can also wear a Nehru jacket or shirt which has a softer style of collar than a Mandarin.

### Necklines
Once again, opt for the softer lines—choose crew necks, drawstring necklines, unbuttoned polo shirts which look softer, and perhaps a "grand-dad collar" (i.e. no collar!). Roll necks look fine too, but not if you have a full round face or a short neck.

## Think About Collars

When you go out shopping for shirts don't just get any old collar or the standard shirt collar that you have always bought. Think a little about your head and neck and face-shape and choose a collar that really complements your own needs—there are lots of choices, so try something different!

#### FOR A LARGER HEAD AND NECK

Collars should counterbalance your facial structure by either softening its dominant lines or strengthening its weak ones. Your collar should frame your face, so a small collar will make a larger head and neck appear even larger—it's all in the scale, so go for larger collars and stay in proportion. If your face is rounded and maybe a little heavy choose a stiff collar with longer points to balance better with your features.

#### FOR LONG NECKS

It is perfectly possible to buy higher sitting collars to disguise an obviously long neck. The neckband is usually wider—go to a specialist shirt shop to find this detail.

#### FOR A WIDE FACE

This type of face needs the collar points to be longer in order for the face to be counterbalanced well.

#### FOR A LONG AND NARROW FACE

The broadly spaced points of a spread collar will counterbalance a long and narrow face.

## Collar Stiffeners

Please buy collars that have the facility to take stiffeners, they will look so much smarter, elegant and sophisticated and an investment in metal stiffeners either brass, silver or even splash out on some gold ones will make you feel very special. The most important thing to remember when putting them in the laundry basket is to remove the stiffeners: they can ruin the washing machine and sometimes ruin the shirt!

## Button Down Collars

These collars are much more relaxed and don't really look their best with a tie, but do look good worn casually open. Worn with a tie they can tend to turn up at the ends. You can find button down soft collars that have a hidden button underneath which holds the points down, but they are never as smart as a crisp, cotton shirt collar with stiffeners inserted.

## Formal Collars

It is a personal matter whether you choose a wing collar or a standard turndown collar dinner shirt. However, men with any excess weight or with shorter necks should not choose a wing collar as this brings the collar right up under the chin, makes the neck look short and the whole image becomes rather squashed. Better to choose the standard turndown shirt collar with a smart bow-tie to give length to the neck.

Choose the bow-tie carefully too. If you do go for a wing collar be careful: a small wing collar is overwhelmed by a large bow-tie, so make sure the tie is in proportion with the collar. The bow-tie should also lie over the wings of the collar, the wings of the collar should be stiff, standing up proudly and not drooping flaccidly over the tie! Hand-tied bow-ties look better than the standard self-stitched and tied versions so do learn to tie it yourself!

## Cuffs and cuff-links

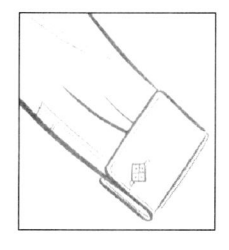

A 'French' or turn back cuff is by far the smartest finish to your shirt. This style necessitates a cufflink closure which in itself can show your good taste and your understanding of dressing well. Gimmicky cuff-links are not advisable in business but a simple 'knot' either in metal or fabric looks neat and there are a myriad of other interesting and stylish cuff-links to choose from.

*Men's Issues*

Short sleeved shirts are worn commonly in hot climates, but can look a little 'unusual' in the British business community – city financial institutions for example would never accept this look.

## TIPS FOR THE VERTICALLY CHALLENGED

If you feel you would like to gain a few inches in perceived height then here are some tips for you.

- Try to wear monotones—i.e. suits, and jackets and trousers in toning colours: this gives an impression of height. A dark jacket with light trousers will form a horizontal line across the body where dark meets light and that tends to give an impression of width and thus shortens the feeling of length.
- Choose slightly higher-heeled shoes and boots to add an inch or two.
- Avoid turn-ups on trousers as these form a horizontal line across the ankle and attract the eye down, shortening the leg.
- Three button suits, either solid or pinstriped, give an impression of height.
- Trousers with a more tapered look or straight cut will lengthen the leg, especially with a crisp crease down the front. Avoid large baggy trousers and trousers that wrinkle around the ankle: one slight "break" is all there should be at the end of the trouser as it meets the shoe.
- Keep your overall silhouette slim and avoid pleats and gathers in trousers: this will give you a slimmer, taller line. Try to achieve a single, unbroken line from your shoulders to the floor: a single-breasted jacket with its one line down the front will work well. NEVER choose a double-breasted suit.
- Pinstripes in suits and any stripe pattern (not too wide) will give an illusion of height. Keep attention on the area from the waist to the top of your head by wearing an interesting tie: this will keep others' attention up high. This area is called the triangle of influence and is the area most seen by others.
- Keep accessories small—paying attention to 'scale' can make a huge difference in how you are perceived.

## Catastrophic Casuals

This section is really aimed at those of you who work in a 'booted and suited' environment. More creative and relaxed environments may accept some of the following, but even those companies who have a dress-down environment may need some form of 'code' that states what can and can't be worn to keep the 'business' environment controlled. In general, avoid:

Denim (it's not professional) unless you work in

- a creative business
- T-shirts with logos
- T-shirts with logos worn under white shirts
- Shorts, unless you work in a hot climate where formal shorts are accepted
- Sleeveless tops
- Visible tattoos
- Any kind of sportswear e.g. trainers, track suits, track bottoms, white socks
- Cowboy boots
- Sandals
- Visible piercings of any sort
- Wearing your shirt outside your trousers, unless in the most relaxed and casual of offices
- A careless attitude to grooming – not shaving,
- unkempt hair, dirty nails
- Visible underpants
- Un-ironed clothing
- Too much personal jewellery
- Mixing your smart black shoes with chinos
- Toting your possessions in carrier bags

A little extreme for the office?

Men's Issues

107

## Business Casual Is ...

## BUSINESS CASUAL IS:

- Immaculate grooming at all times, no matter what the dress code is.
- Clothes which are laundered and pressed and in good repair, that have a modern style. Please think twice about wearing a blazer—it really is now a 1970's item of clothing, perfect for the golf club, sailing club or regatta, but looking dated in the 21st Century. Wear one if your client wears one!
- Smedley cotton and fine knitted polo shirts and sweaters.
- For trousers, think chinos, cords, linen, wool blend, cotton and moleskins.
- Sports jackets in fine wools and cotton and/or linen blends are very suitable and you can also consider reefer-style waist length jackets in cotton. A leather or suede jacket is also good looking—as long as it is clean!
- Good quality round or v-necked tee-shirts without logos which can look good under jackets.
- Good quality cotton casual shirts, soft-collared, button-down and collarless.
- Casual dock-sider shoes and slip-ons.
- Leather belts (to match) of any sort.

Relaxed and careless dressing can often give the wrong impression and attention to simple things like the length of a tie can make a huge difference to the way you present yourself! Ties end on the buckle – not above or below!

**Notes:**

To improve and move on I will ...

Date:_____

## Chapter 6

*"Blessed are the flexible for they shall not be bent out of shape"*. Anon

## Colour Matters!

**colour**

**UNDERSTANDING COLOUR**

Colour has a deep impact on society. Red is often used as a sign of danger, as it has the highest vibration of all colours: the eye sees it before any other colour as it reaches the retina faster than all the others. It can also cause aggression as it raises blood pressure, quickens the pulse and thus makes breathing faster. Orange is an appetite stimulant—e.g. fish fingers are coated in orange breadcrumbs to encourage children to eat them; they would probably not enjoy plain white fish fingers. Blue is cooling, and

Green is calming and balancing, often used in Doctors' surgeries to calm patients while waiting. Colour is being used more and more in alternative therapies, and it is well known that we can see only part of the true colour spectrum. Rather like sound vibrations that only dogs can hear, there are colour vibrations that we can't see.

In my opinion, the right colour is **vital**. The right colour worn close to your face, man or woman, gives your skin a lift, brings out the tones of your own colouring to its best advantage and a sparkle to your eyes. Colour is often thought to be a fluffy, girly, thing, but understanding the colours that suit you best and having a colour consultation with an expert consultant will benefit you enormously. There is a 'real world' benefit to understanding colour in this context.

You need to understand what colours suit you best and how to wear them. In the following paragraphs I will try to explain the different groups of colours and why they suit certain types better than others, but all this is just a guide. I never say you must not wear those colours that are not in your range. What I am suggesting is that if you happen to like those colours, then wear them by all means, but not next to the face. Find a garment in the 'right' colour, like a scarf, shirt or turtleneck, to wear next to the face, thus extending the distance by one article between your face and the 'wrong' colour.

You will find that some image consultants refer to colour in 4 seasons, spring, summer, autumn and winter. This is formula used since the 1970's, but I prefer to break the colour ranges into 6 sets. Each set has a primary set of colour types, and most people will have secondary colour types taken from another set which then allows you more choice. There is even the possibility of having a third set in some cases.

First, let me explain the constituents of colour:

Every colour comes in three parts:

1. Depth or Intensity of Colour.
2. Clarity
3. Undertone

## Depth

'Depth' does not mean 'dark'. 'Depth' means the amount of saturated colour in any given colour. For example a strong Royal Blue is 'Deep', a strong rich yellow is 'Deep', Black (actually, not technically a colour) is obviously Deep, and strangely, so is White (again, not a real 'colour') that is saturated with white and cannot be any more white than white. This is a hard concept to understand at first, but bear with me!

At the other end of the scale from Deep is 'Light'. If you imagine you poured a bucket of water into a bucket of Royal Blue paint, the colour would become light blue, and this is how we think of the 'lighter' colours—more like pale watercolour than their Deep alternative.

Deep ———————————— Medium ———————————— Light

## Clarity

'Clarity' means exactly what it says, the clarity of the colour, the pureness and clearness of the colour, whether it is bright emerald green or bright pink.

So, at one end of the scale you have clear bright colour, and at the other end, imagine you have added grey paint to the bright colour. By the time you reach the end of the scale, the emerald green has now become sage green and the pink is now antique rose, or dusty pink—this is called 'Muted'.

Bright ———————————— Medium ———————————— Muted

## Undertone

Undertone is exactly what it says. It is the mix of colours that show through your skin, yellow or blue, that is to say, warm or cool. This is based on the amount of Melanine (blue-brown) or Carotene (clear to yellow-orange) in your skin. If you have more of the third factor, Haemoglobin, which is the red pigment in blood, the more rosy you will appear, and therefore the cooler your colouring will be (pink being a cool colour as it has a lot of blue in it). Melanine and Carotene are also responsible for the colour of your hair and eyes. Someone with a lot of Carotene will probably be red-haired with freckles and someone with a lot of Melanine in their undertone is likely to have darker skin and hair. Once you understand these facts, you will swiftly recognise the cool or warm features of people's skin.

Warm ──────────────── Medium ──────────────── Cool

So here we have the six varieties of colour, Deep, Light, Bright, Muted, Warm and Cool.

## Black Skin

People with black or very deep brown skins will obviously have Deep as their primary colour type, but they can also add to this basic colour the Bright colourway. This is possible when their skin is paler than their hair and eyes, they can also have a secondary Muted colourway because, if there is little contrast between their skin and hair and eyes, the effect is to show a mellow softness all round.

If there is a hint of warmth in black skin such as a golden brown sheen, this can be thought of as Deep and Warm. Some dark-skinned people have an almost blue-ish tinge to their skin, and sometimes grey hair, so here you have Deep and Cool working together.

## Colour Types in Action

So, now we know what colour is, let's see what colour you might be.

Are you a Deep Person? Dark eyed, dark haired and with medium to dark skin tones

Are you Light? Pale eyes, they could be blue, green or mixes of these colours, light brown, blonde or ash blonde hair, with medium skin tones.

Are you Bright? As here – coloured eyes in all shades except browns and hazels, and dark hair and contrasting skin tones

This is your author! But bright in colour-type, with dark hair and blue eyes, and an obvious contrast between skin and hair.

*Colour Matters!*

Perhaps you are Muted. With hair, skin and eyes in a very similar tone, hair blonde or light brown, brown eyes or dark coloured eyes, and medium to deep skin tones.

Warm is the next colour. Typically you would have red or tones of red in your hair, or be a strawberry blonde. Eyes can be brown, hazel or brightly coloured, and skin is generally quite pale and freckled.

Finally let's hear it for Cool! The Queen is the best example here, grey hair, blue eyes and pale skin.

So that's where the expression Queen of Cool came from!

See if you can recognise what you are from these 6 colourways. You will have a primary colour; see if you have a secondary or even a third as well. And don't forget you can always change your colours to be what you would like, by dying your hair and/or wearing coloured contact lenses. We also lose colour pigment as we age and some people become progressively 'cooler' as hair becomes grey and eyes paler.

Once you have decided what your primary colour type is, you will be able to choose from the colour ranges that suit that type best.

These are recommended colour ranges in each colour Set:

| DEEP Neutrals | BRIGHT Neutrals | WARM Neutrals |
|---|---|---|
| Accent Colours | Accent Colours | Accent Colours |
| LIGHT Neutrals | MUTED Neutrals | COOL Neutrals |
| Accent Colours | Accent Colours | Accent Colours |

## Colour in Business

It is useful to understand how important colour can be in business as well as in everyday life. If you choose the appropriate colours to your situation

*Colour Matters!*

and your environment, you can put yourself on the front foot when it comes to negotiating both with your peers and with clients.

A darker suit, worn either by men or women, gives much more authority and impact. Darker colours add gravitas to your look and, especially when the jacket is done up, can be quite 'closed' and 'unapproachable'. However you will never be seen as an easy target dressed that way! These dark colours apply to colours such as dark grey, black and navy blue, so, if you want to be seen as more open to approach, grey and medium tones are more effective.

If you think of the colour that suits you best in terms of 'highlights', you can soften a harder darker look by wearing a shirt and tie or blouse under the jacket that gives more lift and light to the face, thus enabling a 'power' look but adding approachability to it. Knowing which colour suits you best will also enable you to find the right 'dark' shade to make the most of your style. By choosing the colour that is most suited to your natural colour, attention will be held by your face, and your whole presentation will be improved.

Wearing the 'right' colour for you is not a vanity. It simply gives a healthier, more vital look and helps you to be perceived in the way you wish.

### How to use the Colour Analysis Chart

If you look at the chart on the next page you will see how to work out your own colour 'type'.

In this instance I would like you to imagine a person who has dark brown hair, pale skin and bright blue eyes. She also has some pink tones in her skin.

On the 'Deep' line because she has dark hair, she falls into the 'deep' category—not as deep as she would be if she were black-haired and black-skinned, but deep nevertheless. Here you would put a cross near the deep end of the scale, but not quite at the furthest end.

(If she were blonde she would be further along the top line nearer the 'Light' end)

Because she has bright blue eyes, she is considered to be towards the 'Bright' end of the next scale down. There is a high contrast between her skin and her hair as well, which adds to this element. So here put a cross in the next line down near to the Bright notation.

The next element to investigate is Undertone. She has pink tones in her skin which is a signal that she has cool colouring (pink being a cool colour).

So what does this mean?
In this instance this particular lady (and it would apply just as much to a man) has a Primary Colour of Bright, a secondary colour of Deep and she has Cool undertones.

This means that she can wear bright colours, and high contrasting tones, too, e.g. black and white, but she should wear colours that are on the cool side of the spectrum, therefore mainly blue and blue-influenced colours.

Have a go at the chart below and put the crosses where you think you belong in each category. Maybe you will have a cross in all three lines, maybe in just two and sometimes you are definitely just one colourway!

There is a lot more to this whole analysis process, and this is just a guide to what can be achieved. A full colour analysis with an expert colour analyst can take a couple of hours and is extremely thorough. A session like this will lead to the client receiving a wallet of colours that will guide them throughout their lives on the best tones and colours for their individual type. It is a very worthwhile thing to do and really makes a huge difference when shopping for clothes and for friends who may want to buy you a gift that suits!

Colour Analysis – See How You Do
Put a cross on each line where you think your colourway applies.

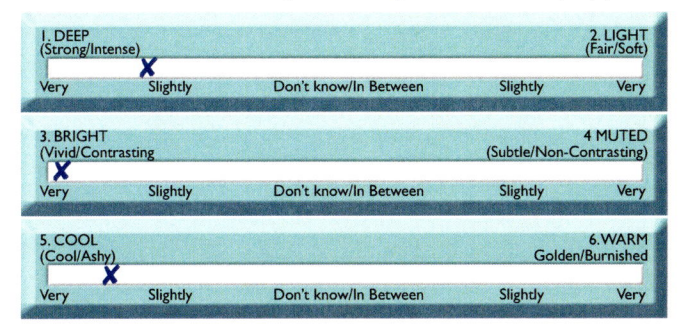

| 1. DEEP (Strong/Intense) | | | | 2. LIGHT (Fair/Soft) |
|---|---|---|---|---|
| Very | **X** Slightly | Don't know/In Between | Slightly | Very |

| 3. BRIGHT (Vivid/Contrasting) | | | | 4 MUTED (Subtle/Non-Contrasting) |
|---|---|---|---|---|
| **X** Very | Slightly | Don't know/In Between | Slightly | Very |

| 5. COOL (Cool/Ashy) | | | | 6. WARM Golden/Burnished |
|---|---|---|---|---|
| Very | **X** Slightly | Don't know/In Between | Slightly | Very |

In the top line, are you deeper or lighter in tone or are you mid-way?

In the middle line does your skin suit brighter clearer tones because you have a high contrast colourway or are your colours more soft and muted and should you perhaps put a cross near the muted end of the scale?

At the bottom, the most important line of all, are you cool in colour, or warm or in the middle? From the result of this line can come the root of all your colour decisions!

Some of you may have only one main colourway, others two, and some of you three! Whatever it is, this chart will give you a guideline to which colours suit you best. Remember, this is only a guideline and a full colour consultation with an expert is truly the best way to achieve your perfect analysis.

### THE PSYCHOLOGICAL ENERGY OF COLOUR

It is a well-known fact that certain colours affect us psychologically, physically and aesthetically. Wearing certain colours can help elicit the desired reaction from people. When you see a red fire engine, lights flashing, siren blaring, your heart starts to race, your eyes dilate and your blood pressure rises. This occurs in a more subtle way in the clothes we wear. For example, if you wear (ladies) a red suit, (gentlemen) a red tie, you will feel more energetic and command attention. Red is only one of the colours with subtle visual powers. There are eleven key colours and I will suggest ways to use each colour.

RED   Red includes true red, burnished red, bright holly red and watermelon red. Light pink shades and fuschia tones are not included in red.

The positive psychological power of red is high energy, danger, passion, vibrancy, confidence, assertion and excitement. Red can also be perceived in a negative way and appear to be aggressive, domineering and threatening.

> Choose Red:   To project authority
> 
> To give yourself a visual boost of energy
> 
> For occasions when you want to draw attention to yourself
> 
> When you want to attract the opposite sex!

| | |
|---|---|
| Avoid Red: | When you are being interviewed on television—it is too 'in your face' |
| | If your position is controversial—it can underline aggression |
| | If you are not prepared to defend your views or position, because this is a very assertive colour |
| | If you are overtired or overstressed—red will make you look more so. |

**YELLOW:** Sunny yellows, bright warm and gold. Lemon yellow is NOT included.

The positive psychological power of yellow is cheerful, filled with anticipation, active and uninhibited, warm, hopeful and hospitable. Negatives include impulsiveness and volatility, cowardice and deceit.

| | |
|---|---|
| Choose Yellow: | To cheer yourself up |
| | When you are in feeling playful |
| | When interacting with children |
| Avoid Yellow: | In a sunny, hot and humid climate—you will feel and look even hotter |
| | When you want to be taken seriously—it is rather a carefree colour |
| | In negotiations—maybe it isn't quite serious enough |

**GREEN:** The colour green includes forest, moss, olive, pine and true greens.

The positive psychological power of green is calm, cool, fresh, friendly, balanced, dependent, nurturing, growth, prosperity and self-reliance. Its negative aspects include envy and immaturity.

| | |
|---|---|
| Choose Green: | to be perceived as calm and dependable |
| | Mixes well with navy blue in a business environment |
| | When tired or stressed—it will calm you |
| Avoid Green: | For evening wear unless emerald and shiny |

**PURPLE:** The colour purple includes medium violets to dark purples, plum, indigo and periwinkle.

The positive psychological power of purple indicates dignity, power, mystery, and wisdom; it is also perceived to be sensitive, passionate and imaginative. On the negative side, purple in certain cultures represents bereavement.

| | |
|---|---|
| Choose Purple: | Works well for the media |
| | For evening elegance |
| | As an alternative choice for a tie in business |
| Avoid Purple: | In some parts of the Asia/Pacific Rim |

**GREY:** Grey includes charcoal, taupes (grey/beige), pewter, medium to dark.

The positive psychological power of grey is neutral, modest and respectable. On the negative side it looks safe, drab, boring and even old!

| | |
|---|---|
| Choose Grey: | For safe business wear—light grey is approachable |
| | In any sort of arbitration as it is a neutral tone |
| | Use as a safe neutral mixed with a bright colour in business |
| Avoid Grey | When you intend to be noticed—in grey you blend into the background |
| | In all creative vocations—it is too dull |
| | When interacting with children—there is no authority |

**BROWN:** Brown includes golden, chocolate, cocoa, and red-browns. The positive psychological power of brown is 'stability', 'earthiness' and 'continuity'. On the negative side, brown can be perceived as boring, safe and unsophisticated ("Never wear brown in town!")

| | |
|---|---|
| Choose Brown: | To open doors of communication—you are not a threat |
| | To appear less intimidating |

Avoid Brown:    For evening wear unless it is a rich velvet

Unless you really want to present a neutral position

Among your peers and colleagues unless you want to blend in.

**ORANGE:**    Orange includes tangerine, peach and pumpkin.

The positive psychological power of orange is enthusiasm, uninhibitedness, fun, vitality and vibrancy; it is also hopeful and hospitable. On the negative side, orange can be perceived as a fad colour or superficial.

Choose Orange:    If you are muted or warm coloured

If you have 'bright' colouring mix with bright flamingo pink for a vibrant look

Avoid Orange:    If you are not happy in a bold colour—you should be bold to wear it!

In most business situations—it shouts too much!

**BLUE:**    Blue includes navy, clear blues, medium blues and royal. Pastel blues and aquas are not included.

The positive power of blue is trustworthiness, strength, control and orderliness. It is also linked with esteem, serenity, tranquillity and truth. On the downside it can be sad and depressing.

Choose Blue:    the darkest blues project the most authority in business

Mid-tone blues work well on television

Mid-tone blues inspire confidence

Avoid Blue:    At a conference of bankers, lawyers or accountants unless you want to blend in!

When working in a creative field such as advertising, design and marketing—it's a bit 'safe'.

**PINK:**    Pink includes both cool and warm hues, mid-tone salmon colours, candyfloss, corals and raspberry pink.

The positive power of pink is non-threatening, accessible, feminine and gentle.

| | |
|---|---|
| Choose Pink: | As a petitioner in a divorce court, if you want the court's sympathy. |
| | In a shirt or blouse to soften a power suit. |
| Avoid Pink: | Women: In a management position unless extremely tailored—it is too fluffy and young as a colour. |
| | Men: Not too strong pink in a shirt, ice pink is acceptable. |
| | In a leadership role—it doesn't have enough gravitas. |
| | Discussing promotion, for the same reason. |

**BLACK:** This is an absence of colour. The positive power of black is sophistication, power, formality dignity and seriousness.

On the negative side, black can be perceived as mournful, lifeless, tragic, gloomy and foreboding.

| | |
|---|---|
| Choose Black: | For funerals as a sign of respect. |
| | For evening events, but wear it blended with other 'lighter' colours e.g. (ladies) jewellery or wraps (men) white or pastel shirts. |
| | For high-power suits. |
| Avoid Black: | Near your face unless you are well tanned. |
| | On television—it can make a dull image. |
| | For happy occasions! |

**WHITE:** Technically and rather surprisingly, in colour terms, white is a deep colour (it can't get any whiter!). It is vibrant and pure, and includes all the soft shades of ivory and soft whites.

The power of white is freshness, cleanliness, youthfulness, and peace. The negative side can seem clinical or neutral.

Choose White as a contrast with dark colours, and avoid it unless your grooming is impeccable. Off-white is best against most complexions, winter (pure) white good in trousers and skirts.

**Notes**

TO IMPROVE AND MOVE ON I WILL ...

DATE:_____

# Chapter 7

*"A minor change can make a major difference"* Anon

## Conveying The Message

### The Power of Personal Marketing

Are you packaged to sell?

Studies show that there are 3 reasons why someone buys you, your product or your services:

You appear HONEST (I feel I can trust you)

You appear KNOWLEDGEABLE (I feel you know what you are doing)

You appear SINCERE (I feel you have my vested interest at heart)

Companies spend billions of dollars in advertising and packaging to make their products more desirable by gaining their customers' attention and confidence and to increase their share of the available market.

People can also be perceived as products. Either you will be bought or the competition will be. Are you packaged to come out the winner?

CREATE YOUR OWN IDENTITY AND CONSTANTLY REINFORCE IT

### Authority

- JACKET: A jacket will always add instant power and authority. Ladies, when asked to present in a senior position, don't rely on a simple blouse or top and skirt or trousers. A smart jacket, sensibly chosen with style and impact will always add impact to your presentation.

- QUALITY: Quality speaks very quietly *and* very loudly. We can all spot quality from the fabric through to the cut, it speaks volumes about your taste and your attention to important detail.
- COLOUR: Darker colours have more power and authority than lighter colours. A buttoned-up jacket can appear closed, so beware the body language here. A lighter colour worn open over a shirt or top is more amenable and approachable. Choose whichever is most appropriate to your particular situation at the time.
- COMFORTABLE AND APPROPRIATE: The clothes you have chosen should not be right or wrong, but appropriate and have 'ease'. Your wardrobe should suit your situation and the people you are with, whether clients or colleagues
- ACCESSORIES: A few quality pieces suited to you and your garments. Bear in mind that the colour of the accessories, jewellery and watches you choose can also influence and affect the overall 'look' e.g. dark people with cool undertones generally suit white gold and silver jewellery, while warmer-toned individuals look good in gold.
- BE CONTEMPORARY and geared to your profession. Watch the movers and shakers in your profession and emulate them.
- COSMETICS: Less is more, and gentlemen, don't overdo the aftershave.
- CONSISTENCY: Every day counts. People only notice the one or two things that you didn't do as well as you should have or could have.

## IMAGE KILLERS

### DRESSING IN AN INCONSISTENT MANNER

In business, as in most other parts of our lives, people expect consistency from you, e.g. promising to do something every week, and always doing it. In a similar vein, if you promote yourself as a smart, elegant professional who is always reliable and consistent, and you turn up one day in scruffy shoes and careless clothes that don't reflect your professionalism, the integrity of your image is lost and can be difficult to regain. Maintain your wardrobe and keep your work clothes for work, not for other uses. Ensure that repairs are done straight away—it is easy just to put the garment back in the cupboard, but when you need it in a rush you'll need to mend it. Make sure this doesn't happen to you!

### Dressing beneath yourself

I have already addressed this to some extent, but I want to stress the point that you should dress for the position above your current position or for the level you wish to join. Be aspirational and be noticed, which you will be if you consistently look smart and capable. Dressing down in an environment that is not necessarily a dress-down business will only result in your being passed over as not being able to match the clients that are bringing in the revenue. Appropriate office clothing is always the best route to take, but beware of overdoing it, too!

If you are at a senior level, it is important that the people below you can look to you for inspiration and leadership. Allowing your personal presentation to slide, even if your company is dress-down in culture, is not a good example.

### Appearing nervous or anxious

Hand-wringing, fiddling with hair, jangling change in your pockets (men), speaking too softly, avoiding eye contact, and fidgeting can all make you seem nervous or anxious, which itself breeds uncertainty by others in your abilities. Nervous energy can communicate fear in an uncomfortable situation. Body language is a large part of building a great brand. Good stance—head up, shoulders back—good eye contact, firm (not painful) handshakes and a clear and honest smile give an appearance of confidence and ability, even if underneath you are less than happy! Don't forget that 55% of that vital first impression includes body language and only 7% to the actual message that you have to give. However, remember that the body signals you are receiving may sometimes be due to an underlying condition. That 'limp lily' handshake may make you think the person is weak, but they may be suffering from arthritis. Someone with their arms folded over their chest in the office may be trying to stay warm, but in a warm room it is a defensive, uninviting message.

### Allowing yourself to be constantly interrupted

If you allow people constantly to interrupt you, you are giving them permission to shut you down, which will give an impression that you lack strength and confidence. Being a good listener is a great thing to be and a skill to learn, but it is definitely not good always to be the listener. Politely stand your ground and make your opinions heard with clarity and consistency.

**POOR DINING AND SOCIAL SKILLS**

'Flash and brash' does not equal 'style and grace'. The basics of good table manners, despite being thought of as rather old fashioned, will make a difference to the way you are perceived when entertaining in a business situation.

It's not just table manners that are important, but social manners, too, and there are many books on the subject. This 'finishing off' of an individual enables you to be more rounded in any social situation and leaves you less likely to drop clangers or end up embarrassed over a social gaffe. Gain acceptance when you get it right, but get it wrong and you're remembered for all the wrong reasons. Do take the time if you feel unsure about the rights and wrongs of modern manners to read through an expert view. I recommend:-

The Times Book of Modern Manners: A Guide through the Minefield of Contemporary Etiquette.

**POOR GROOMING**

Of course this just isn't acceptable in business. Enormous care must be taken over personal hygiene, as nothing gives a worse impression than unwashed hair, unclean hands and nails, poor skin and discoloured teeth and, in extreme cases, halitosis due to lack of dental hygiene.

**DO YOU HAVE A WINNING SMILE?**

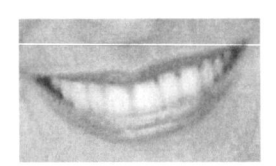

Do you know that nineteen out of twenty people suffer from gum disease at some point in their life? That makes gum disease the most common disease in the world! Not only is this worrying, but according to statistics one in four people have bad breath. Oh dear.

How are your teeth? Do you smile with confidence and ease? It's a big part of your personal brand, helping you win friends and influence people. Do you make a point of visiting your dental hygienist and your dentist regularly? To add further stats to this, 2/3$^{rd}$ of the population who regularly brush their teeth, both night and morning, still suffer from visible plaque deposits and this neglect can lead to gum disease and, horror of horrors, loss of teeth. This build-up of bacterial plaque can even shorten life expectancy when this bacteria is regularly recycled through our bloodstreams. It's an awful thought.

Badly kept teeth can add years to your age, and they are one of the first features people look at. Teeth lose their brightness as you age, become chipped and even ground down, amalgam fillings can add to their dullness too, so take a good look at them, from not just the front-on point of view but with a mirror, from the side view too, then honestly evaluate how they appear.

So, what can we do if they are not perfect? Well, obviously apart from the regular dental check-ups, we can take great care to reduce plaque through using plaque-revealing tablets which really do show up the areas of teeth which you may not be brushing on a regular basis and there are an enormous number of options available to us, including non-surgical procedures which can enhance the look of our teeth and our smiles.

Veneers (thin porcelain which is bonded to the natural teeth) crowns, bridges implants and tooth whitening are all available to improve and strengthen our teeth. Invisible braces are now being commonly utilised to move teeth back into shape in new high tech advances and, although I never advocate facelifts or any invasive surgery, it is even possible in extreme cases to have a dental 'facelift' that works by restoring the teeth, and lifting jawlines which can take years off a patient's face.

Of course cost could become an issue here as not much of this new technology is cheap. The one procedure that is becoming very commonplace however, and which isn't too expensive is tooth whitening. Beware however of overdoing this treatment as teeth which have been unrealistically whitened can look quite dazzling and extremely unnatural leading to your smile being noticed for all the wrong reasons! So if you decide to go down this route, do keep the look natural and not neon!

## Marketing the Brand

So what is 'marketing' if not 'influencing'? Every product that is marketed is being offered as something you need. You are influenced by its cost, its shape, its effectiveness; your feelings about it are influenced by the advertisers through your emotions. We are led to buy through what we feel we need, or must have to improve our status.

So why shouldn't this work for you as an individual product? To be perceived as desirable and powerful and essential? Your Personal Brand will influence how people feel about you and help you to become king or queen in your own arena.

In order to present a brand effectively you need to understand your own 'marketing mix'. You are not building a faux-image for the outside world, you are building your brand to show the world your USP, your strengths, skill and passions, and through your consistency of actions the business and personal wealth will follow.

The product is you, "ID-YOU©", call it what you will—your core values, experience, temperament and personality. Once your vision is clear, and you have a personal brand that is broadcasting exactly what you are and what you have to sell, use the five 'P's' to identify and constantly reinforce your brand—Price, Position, Place, Packaging and Promotion.

### The Price
If you are in employment, make sure that you see your true value by researching the market value for the job and ask for that value: don't undervalue yourself. Entrepreneurs need to see it differently: if people think they are getting a cheap product, they will be wary; higher fees have their own psychology that expects a quality offering. Research, research, research to find out what people are paying and will pay. It's better to offer something free as a 'taster' than cheapen your offering with discounted low prices which, in the long run, won't be appreciated. Fee integrity is all.

### The Place
How and where you sell yourself alongside your competitors is what you need to understand. What is your speciality and where are you going to find the opportunities you seek? Find a marketplace first for your talent

then build **ID-YOU**© to fit whether it will be, on the outside, booted and suited, or more casual. Whatever you choose, it must communicate what you stand for in order to grow both your individual and corporate success.

### The Packaging

Packaging is the main ingredient to being perceived well on first meeting and making an excellent first impression. Get the packaging right and you will be well on the way to communicating and building a winning personal brand. Tap into the power of non-verbal communication (NVC). People will always believe the evidence of their own eyes at first sight. If someone looks professional, we are apt to believe that person until they let us down. At first sight we judge people through the non-verbal communication skills they present.

It is important to remember, when you first walk in to a room the person/people in there make a subconscious snap judgement about you within 20 seconds. 55% of this first impression is solely to do with your clothing, general appearance, and body language. The next percentage, still a large one at 38%, is based on your voice alone and you still haven't said anything substantial.

If your 'packaging' (remember that you are the product here) is confusing and hard to understand, your message, which is only 7% of the first impression that remains, will not be heard. As I mentioned earlier, this is sometimes called 'the halo' effect. When your visual message is positive, people will assume that other aspects will be equally positive. Unfortunately, if your visual message is negative, the new customer or client may not spend the time to discover the talented person inside.

Understanding your own personal presentation, what suits you in terms of colours and styles and being appropriate to the situation at hand, will put you on the front foot in all first impressions with your clients and peers and give you that 'unfair advantage' over your competitors.

Colour is often thought to be a fluffy, girly thing. Far from it! Understanding which colours suit you best and having a personal colour consultation with an expert consultant will benefit you enormously. The psychological benefits of choosing the right colours have been shown to be extraordinarily accurate and psychologically telling; you will be perceived to be healthy, alert and open to discussion (not to mention better-looking), rather than closed, dominant or aggressive! There is a real-world benefit to understanding colour and what it can do for you.

### THE WRONG IMPRESSION

There is, in fact, a huge link between appearance and personal identity. Women generally find it easier to apply to themselves than most men; some men even find it trivial. Trivial it isn't. Examples of bad style issues in men are comb-over hairstyles, curly collars, badly fitting, tired clothes, missing buttons, the 2" of hairy ankle showing over sloppy short socks, a lack of personal freshness. For women, examples are holes in tights, down-at-heel shoes, inappropriate clothing and too much or no make-up. All these are impact killers and can make the difference between being seen and not seen. People who take no interest in their personal appearance will find that others take no interest in them! Yes, it seems superficial, but in our current image-obsessed community it is a fact of life and ignored at your peril.

### THE PERCEPTION

Be perceived to be beneficial. If you are talking to a group of executives in finance say, better to be appropriate and be on their level. Nothing will make a group of house-to-house salespeople in their smart casual clothing more resentful than having a super-smart speaker who will inevitably be seen as speaking down to them. So appropriateness is all. Match the clients and be perceived by them as understanding their positions and having an answer they can equate to.

### THE PROMOTION

"People won't buy it if they can't see it". It is good to have some promotion techniques for building awareness. People must know who you are, what you stand for, what you have to offer and how to find you.

How visible are you? How many people see you and can pass on their opinions of your good value and the benefits you offer. How influential are these people and how can you influence them?

Build up your own brand loyalty: "once tried, often re-purchased with no further advertising". Even now General Electric in the US is still rated 2$^{nd}$

best kitchen blender 20 years after they stopped making them! People like to buy from other people with whom they feel a connection. That is what lies at the heart of the Personal Branding phenomenon.

Don't forget the external elements that also add to your branding. Logos, business cards, vehicle livery and premises. An image audit of your premises is often the first step in assessing your business. Are staff smoking outside the front door? Are company cars in the car park clean? Was coffee served to visitors in a china cup and saucer or a polystyrene cup? Is the receptionist smart and aware, or filing her nails? Is the reception area clean and tidy and not piled high with boxes? How is your voice-mail? etc., etc.

### Your differentiator

What have you got that your contemporaries and competitors don't have? What is your Unique Selling Point? Are you the first, the best, the only, the most unusual, the cheapest, the most expensive, the most amusing, the most innovative etc.

Again, ask yourself these questions:

> What do I stand for?
> What am I known for?
> How can I stand out?
> How do I add value?
> What is my visibility rating?

These elements should help you find your own particular USP.

Which leaves us with the external elements of your personal brand

> Your appearance
> Your clear voice,
> Your body language,
> Your listening skills,
> Your verbal message,
> Your presence and impact.

Good grooming matters, too. You could be giving directions to the fabled New Forest Diamond Mines, but if people are reeling back from halitosis or BO, they won't be listening to your wonderful message!

Your non-verbal communication + your message = impact.

So, to reiterate, recognise your own USP, then package, promote yourself and develop your own personal brand. Focusing on the package, your impact and your personal presentation will take you from the mundane to the exciting.

What are the exceptions to excellent personal branding?

>   When you are hired purely because of your connections.
>   When you are hired only because of your skills set.
>   When you are hired solely because of your knowledge.

Who can afford to ignore the rules?

>   The very powerful,
>   The very beautiful,
>   The very rich who have nothing to prove,
>   The very poor who have nothing to lose.

## SPACE

*"Persuasion is often more effective than force."* Aesop

One of the most important non-verbal forms of communication is 'space'. How often have you felt uncomfortable in a crowded Tube train or elevator when someone is standing or sitting too close to you?

We all have our own boundaries, a sort of invisible bubble all around, and any uninvited penetration of this bubble can leave us feeling angry, violent or looking to escape.

You have probably noticed that, when eating at a table for two, if your companion puts something on 'your' side of the table it can lead to your feeling uncomfortable and uneasy. If you regularly visit a restaurant you can become quite familiar with a particular table, and if this table is not available next time you arrive, once again you can feel quite uneasy.

You claim 'ownership' of tables and cupboards at home by placing favourite possessions on and in them. Your car is another good example of your space zone. If you are cut up by another driver, your reaction is the same as if that person had intruded upon your personal space without consent.

Men tend to stand further away from each other than women, and couples in conversations stand close. However, if one of the parties is not particularly interested in the conversation they will move away a little, distancing themselves.

People who grow up in the countryside need more space than those raised in country towns and they in turn need more space than those born in cities.

The space between people can be divided up into zones:

- The intimate zone—an area approximately zero to 18" from our bodies. This space is heavily guarded and permission to enter this space is highly selective.
- The personal zone—this extends from one and a half feet to four feet from the body, and is further divided into 2 zones, close personal and far personal.

- The social zone—from 4 to 12 feet apart, usually the distance stood between business people who are not too familiar with each other. Again, this zone is divided into 2, the close zone and the far zone, dependant upon familiarity and social standing.

In the office, space is used to divide staff from visitors, e.g. a receptionist may have a windowed room for receiving visitors, but the visitors do their waiting far enough away that she can continue her work.

The final zone is the public zone, anything over twelve feet, and is common for informal gatherings or when people are speaking to groups they know.
(With thanks to Dr. Edward Hall).

## ETIQUETTE

*"People may doubt what you say, but they always believe what you do".*
Anon.

I expect you think 'finishing school' when you hear the word 'etiquette', but in this instance etiquette has nothing to do with finishing school. It means a set of guidelines for everyday ethical living, respecting those around you by respecting their values. Building rapport and understanding through your consideration of other people's feelings is an essential part of your Personal Brand.

This is by no means an exhaustive look at the subject of etiquette but a guideline to capture the essence of the subject. Having good manners and consideration for others is the polish that takes the 'rough edges' away and can make the difference between being noticed and not being noticed.

People make a note of poor manners and impolite behaviour and it will reflect not only on you, but also on your company. Strangely enough, if you behave impeccably and ensure everyone you are entertaining is having a great time, your manners probably won't be noticed, but the fact that everyone enjoyed themselves will, reflecting favourably on everyone around. Good etiquette creates a harmonious environment and shows you at your personal best.

### CORPORATE ENTERTAINMENT

'Flash and brash' does not mean style and grace', being able to entertain corporately gracefully and with sophistication is a wonderful asset. Table manners are important. Sadly these days a lot of families have never been introduced to good table manners. Some families never eat together, but take snacks and meals on the run or on their laps on a tray. In a formal sit-uation it is important to know which knife and fork to pick up, which is the right glass for which wine, how to add condiments (salt, pepper, mustard etc.) to your dish, or how to eat a bread roll correctly—yes, there is a right and a wrong way! Knowing how to choose the right sort of meal to eat when entertaining clients. Do you really want the hassle of spaghetti when trying to look cool and sophisticated?! Would you order an uncut grapefruit at a breakfast meeting, then splash people with the juices as you dig in and attempt to break it apart?! If you were presented with an artichoke would you know how to eat it?

These are just a few examples you will find in the minefield that is waiting out there for the unwary, and if you are unsure about the rights and wrongs of table etiquette then I suggest you find some further reading material (there is a list of further reading at the end of this book) to study, or wait for my next book which will be addressing this particular subject!

Table manners aren't complicated social savoire faire and proper dining skills may pale in comparison to what is happening on the balance sheet, but they will be noticed by your business colleagues, and if you are not interested in the rules, then perhaps you should steer clear of corporate entertainment.

Who cares about the waiting staff? You should. Politeness and consideration for the waiting staff in a restaurant, and receptionists, bell-boys and porters in hotels, is part of your Personal Brand. They are doing a job and expect some respect for it. Dealing rudely with these people will only make you look boorish and uncouth, not at all sophisticated.

The opposite side of the coin is that if they recognise you as someone they see regularly who tips well and treats them with respect and care, you will reap the benefits in getting the best table, the best room, the best service, all of which can only add to your prestige in the eyes of your guests.

I consider it a good investment to take the time to get to know the Maitre d' in your local restaurant. If he is worth his salt, he will give you the best table and ensure you have the best service throughout your visit. A good tip is a great investment and should be given discreetly either on arrival or on departure.

If you are lucky enough to be in a position to entertain your clients at classical British venues, e.g. Glyndebourne (opera), Ascot (racing), St. Andrews (golf), Henley (rowing) or Cowes (sailing), do make sure that you know the form! Find out what is expected of you, as well as of the venue, and prepare yourself and your guests for the experience. Check out the facilities, make sure that your guests have received detailed arrival instructions (they may even like a car laid on), and make sure they know the dress code—nothing worse than putting yourself or your guests on the back foot by being incorrectly dressed. Don't ply your guests or yourself with too much alcohol, find out their food preferences and make sure they are contacted the day before to ensure they have all the information they need. Arrive early, no matter what the occasion! You should be there to greet everyone: nothing loses more respect than being late, especially on a regular basis. It is also good to have a table plan and know the correct form as to who sits where, e.g. your principal guest on your right etc.

If you are a guest write a handwritten 'thank you' note—it is a gracious thing to do and takes no great effort. A letter written by your secretary on your behalf, or signed 'pp' by her could be considered very rude. It is this attention to detail which will pay dividends in the long run.

Generally in business you should respect the rank and order within the company. Larger companies in particular have a hierarchy; find out what it is and what is required of you.

Respect others' privacy; respect their personal space and don't overstep the mark.

Avoid office gossip. Don't get pulled in—it can have disastrous consequences.

Generally try to think of yourself as an ambassador for yourself and your organisation and you shouldn't go wrong.

## Your Public Image

*"If it looks like a duck, walks like a duck, talks like a duck – it probably needs a little longer in the microwave."* Anon

In business a professionally-taken photograph is a must-have.

Whether you are going to use a photograph in your own business collateral—company brochure, website, speaker profile, or as a page in your employer's annual report or brochure, it is essential to have an elegant photograph taken by a good professional photographer. You should have a choice of black and white and colour pictures, at least 2-3 rolls taken on film, or a series of digital pictures on a disc, and these should be in a printable format (usually jpg), 300 psi resolution for printing, or 72 psi for electronic use.

Don't rely just on the photographer either! You should have taken great care of your appearance—recently cut or styled hair, teeth shining (yes, you could have them whitened!), ladies not too much make-up. If the photographer is good at his job, he will advise you on what works and what doesn't on film. Gentlemen, make sure you have shaved very recently and you too could take a powder compact with you –a little press of powder on forehead and cheeks will take away any greasy shine which isn't so noticeable in daylight, but under lights is very clear. Television reporters always wear makeup, whether male or female.

You should also take along a selection of clothes. Not all clothing is photogenic and you will also want to be aware of the kind of image you want to present of yourself; a 'suited and booted' look, 'the true professional', or a more casual relaxed shot. Even better, have both: then you will have a choice of which kind of photo to use dependent upon its ultimate location. For a professional look, a dark suit, light shirt and simple tie is best for men, and a dark business suit for women, too, with a lighter blouse. Keep jewellery to a minimum. Be sure that you brief the photographer about the usage of the pictures. He may decide to shoot studio shots, which are ultimately very controllable, or outdoor pictures which can be more relaxed. Again, both may be a good idea.

Don't rely on a computer-retouched photograph as this can be expensive and obvious.

On the day, don't be rushed, allow plenty of time to do the pictures. This is something you should be doing every 2-3 years, especially if there are substantial changes in your appearance, and a rushed job will most likely not come up to expectations.

It is also a good idea to have your session earlier rather than later in the day, when you are at your freshest.

If you want to be photographed without your glasses try to wear contacts or take your glasses off if at all possible several hours beforehand to minimise the nose marks that so often signal a glasses wearer.

Remember, if you are using a photograph that is substantially out of date the difference between vain hope and reality simply draws attention to the passage of time.

## The Golden Rules of Good Business Manners

## I M P A C T!

- **I** = INTEGRITY
- **M** = MANNERS
- **P** = PERSONALITY
- **A** = APPEARANCE
- **C** = CONSIDERATION
- **T** = TACT

### Integrity

This is the absolute 'bedrock' of your brand. Your integrity delivers to the world an honest, caring and reliable person. If you live with integrity as your greatest moral value, you can run your working life, as well as your private life, with honesty and truth and you will never have a problem with the other criteria. A vital point to remember is that a reputation for integrity is slowly gained but lost in a flash should you become inconsistent.

### Manners

Your manners are paramount to indicate to the people you work with and live with that you will always act correctly and fairly with them, that you have their interests at heart and that you will develop a relationship with them where they can feel comfortable in their day-to-day interactions with you.

### Personality

Your unique personality is what you bring to your business and private life. In business, be excited but not emotional; be irreverent but not disloyal; be fun to work with but not careless and, finally, self-aware but not pompous.

### Appearance

Your appearance has been covered in some detail in this book and it is a vital part of your Personal Brand. Make sure that it doesn't become a liability and that it never lets you down.

## Consideration

Be considerate with everyone. It costs nothing and reaps huge rewards. It underlines nearly all our actions in business. Care and forethought are the basic principles of consideration and your sensitivity to others' feelings will mark you out as kind, distinctive and memorable.

**Emergency Grooming Kit for Your Desk Drawer**

*"The inventory goes down the elevator every night"* Fairfax Cone

- Hair care products
- Hair and clothes brushes
- Spare tie (m)
- Toothbrush, paste and floss
- Body spray
- Deodorant
- Concealer
- Breath Spray
- Nail file
- Eye drops for red or tired eyes
- Travel size sewing kit
- Clear varnish for ladders in tights (f)
- Spare tights (f)

## Final Words

I think it is important to realise that even though we have talked about core values, perception of you by others, your goals and visions and loads of detail on 'packaging the product', other factors need to be taken into consideration.

One of these areas is health. We talked about your core values but what else comes out of you and that reflects on the outside? Your health. If you don't take care of yourself, if you don't eat properly, have enough sleep or take good preventive care of yourself, it can be seen in your eyes, hair, body and productivity at work.

Another area is fitness. You may not have the most perfectly proportioned body in the world, but if you are fit and toned you will have a great look. You will be able to handle stress and have more visible energy that will invigorate you and those around you. I really believe that exercise is the 'fountain of youth'—even if you are not in the first flush of youth don't give up. Start now. Exercise and grow fitter—it will make a huge difference to the way you feel and the added benefit will be that your clothes will look better on you, too.

The third point is education. You don't need to have been to university but you do need to be well versed in reading, writing and speaking the English language. I hear frequently from companies that their people find it difficult to communicate both orally and via the written word. Accent is unimportant if what you are saying is interesting—in fact a regional accent can add cachet to the spoken word. What is important is that what you say is clear, relevant and stimulating. Our whole lives are a learning process and anyone who is not interested in learning more could be perceived as boring.

Finally, get out there and enjoy yourself! Some of us really enjoy working, but it is still vital to take the time out to mix with friends and family. Enjoy the journey through your life, learn as much as you can from all around you and enjoy your experiences. I wish you every success.

**Notes**

TO IMPROVE AND MOVE ON I WILL ...




DATE:_____

# Recommended Reading List

| | |
|---|---|
| Men's Wardrobe | Kim Johnson Gross and Jim Stone |
| 7 Habits of Highly Effective People | Steven Covey |
| The Secrets of Communication | Peter Thomson |
| The Ultimate Business Presentation Book | Andrew Leigh |
| Gentlemen – a Timeless Fashion | Bernhard Roetzel |
| The New Professional Image | Susan Bixler |
| BodyTalk at Work | Judi James |
| Presenting to Win | Khalid Aziz |
| NLP at Work | Sue Knight |
| Walking Tall | Lesley Everett |
| Style Directions for Men | Carol Spenser |
| Style Directions For Women | Carol Spenser |
| Purple Cow | Seth Godin |

# CHAPTER 8

## WHAT PEOPLE SAY ABOUT CHANGING GEAR

### What people say about Changing Gear:

#### Corporate References:

*"Tessa's involvement during the past 18 months represents a significant investment by the business … the investment has been not only significant but worthwhile and is seen to be an integral part of the whole Relationship Management programme which for me is a measure of its success."*

Senior Manager
Sales and Relationship Management Training
HSBC BANK Plc

*"Thank you for your tremendous contribution to the GRM Skills Programme over the last 18 months. This programme has been one of the most successful learning and development initiatives we have run and is having visible benefits in the business."*

Senior Divisional Director
CIBM/HSBC

*"Tessa Hood is an inspiration. Her recent training session with British Airways, aimed at women wishing to return to the Corporate World of Work, was informative, professionally delivered and extremely well pitched for the target audience.*

*She engaged instantly with the group, addressed their needs and essentially re-injected them with the self-confidence they needed to be able to tackle the challenges of the workplace. Tessa has the unique ability to communicate at all levels and with all people. She is incredibly sensitive to her target audience and can adapt appropriately.*

*I would highly recommend both Tessa and her company "Changing Gear" as one of the most professional Image Consultancy companies I have worked with."*

Languages Project Manager
British Airways

*"Thanks for a superb session yesterday at our Guillemont Park offices. Your 50 minutes, with Q&A, was a very worthwhile experience for our audience who have gone away with food for thought.*

*I particularly liked the way you brought the whole audience into the discussion. It was also enjoyable to watch you draw in our contingent of student interns and to see them respond, and I have no doubt this will benefit them in many ways when they leave Sun."*

Volume Services Program Manager
Sun Microsystems

*"It has been a long time since I attended an Open Forum, however, I am really pleased that I did. I found it really informative and interesting. The speaker, Tessa, was excellent!"*

Manager GAM Limited

*"Brilliant! Tessa did a great job especially including all the male aspects as often these things are very female orientated. I was impressed at how many men attended."*

Manager, GAM Limited

*"Will GAM be offering any follow up sessions with Tessa Hood? I think a lot of people could benefit not only on the clothes side but also how we present ourselves and our day-to-day manners. Thanks for organising"*

Manager, GAM Limited

*"Well done!!!!!! Thanks so much for today. I think you have bowled us over".*

Training Manager, GAM Limited

"Thank you so much for the time and effort you have put into the work you've done with me. The help and advice you gave has really given me a push to move away from my comfort zone. During our time together you helped me understand why I didn't like some clothes and really did like others. The London trip was the best though. The research you did beforehand and the help on the day were superb. The savings you made must have more than made up for your fee, probably double.

Last Friday we did the photo shoot for our new website and it won't need a caption to say which photo is the Managing Director."

Managing Director
Oris Limited

" I appreciated your excellent advice and support last week. I found it very interesting to understand just what works for me and WHY it does or doesn't. That has had quite an impact on my shopping behaviour: now when I go into a shop, I make a bee-line for the right colours and only try on clothes if both the cut and the colour are right for me. Previously I kept getting fed up with clothes shopping because I tried on so much that didn't work for me that I ended up either buying the wrong thing or being very frustrated without a purchase. I'm also so much more confident in my own style and how I wear my clothes. And that can't be all bad, as I got quite a few compliments about my looks this week."

Treasury Specialist
Aspect Capital

"I have consulted with Tessa Hood of Changing Gear recently in connection with a thorough review of my business positioning and future strategy.

I first heard her speak at a private seminar and was impressed by the thoroughness and 'down to earth' practicality that she brought to an intensely personal and subjective subject.

I was so impressed by her mastery of the subject of personal branding and perception that I invested my own money in consulting her.

My initial perceptions were reinforced by the depth of her understanding and intuitive perception. If one keeps an open mind, she will give great insight and depth of information within a short period of time.

*Her consultation was supported by an excellent personalised workbook, this is a tour de force of the elements needed to understand your brand positioning and reinforce the positive aspects by presentation, including grooming, style and posture.*

*I would not hesitate to recommend Tessa and plan to use her both in my next business venture and to advise my children as they enter the workplace."*

Entrepreneur,
Financial Markets

*"Thanks so much for a great presentation today. You scored a 5/5 on the feedback form with everyone - and lots adding more saying how good you were and how they enjoyed hearing you."*

Ladies That Lunch Business Network.

*"Thank you for opening my eyes to the power of the image and personal brand. What you said has definitely stuck in my mind. I'm starting to see things differently, a real revelation! Keep up the excellent work."*

Managing Director
Nova Consulting Limited

*"I enjoyed your presentation to us at The Executive Network which I felt was excellent and delivered with real aplomb to a potentially difficult audience – needless to say you had us all wrapped around your little finger. Your message is critically important for us all."*

Management Consultant

*"I much enjoyed meeting you last night at The Executive Network, and wanted especially to tell you how much your talk impressed me as it was full of good insights and tips, well-constructed, powerfully delivered and amusing to the end. Thanks!"*

Company Director

*"If you are selling at board level then you seriously need to work with Tessa to stack the cards in your favour. I now understand what will add to my personal impact and perceived value.*

*Image and first impressions is especially important in my business. Tessa* showed me that dressing for success need not cost any more. Indeed, I more than saved her fees on following her recommendations for my wardrobe. She's great fun too!"

Managing Director,
Pro Excellence Ltd.,

"I really enjoyed the course you ran the other week and have been brutally eliminating all my old clothes from my wardrobe!"

Team Leader
BUPA International

## Personal References

"Tessa has a wealth of experience. A well informed and thorough professional she radiates warmth and sincerity. Tessa has so much to offer any professional person needing that something extra to make their mark in an ever increasingly focused world where appearances matter and influence."

Tony Craddock
Entrepreneur Financial Markets

" I wish I'd 'found' her sooner! Tessa's approach is warm and friendly, Her keen artist's eye underlines the business-like and practical manner in which she addresses one's problems. Her visit is like a breath of fresh air!"

Mrs. E.M. Weybridge

"Since seeing Tessa, & gaining a whole load of confidence, men turn their heads in my direction. Not that I'm planning on changing men or anything, but it doesn't half do your ego a power of good!"

Sue King
Safari Park Conservationist
African Wildlife Safaris. South Africa

"I'm not sure that I'm very representative of Tessa's usual clientele – as a new mum at 48 and a student of landscape gardening – but then, one of her strengths is an apparent effortless ability to make the most of anyone – from visually disabled career ladies needing a boost to the next rung, to builders looking for the image to go with a glamorous night out on the town!

*What People Say About Changing Gear*

*After an initial wardrobe clear out at home in Paris Tessa arranged a tight schedule of pampering and shopping in London, tailored to my exact needs. It was amazing how an objective assessment of my appearance could so clearly bring out my character.*

*I think this is the essence of Tessa's ability – she seems to be able to work out who you are, and, in the context of your lifestyle, help you look and feel your best".*

Nicky Turc
La Celle St. Cloud, Paris.

# Appendix

## The Real Game's Personal Values Workbook

**INTRODUCTION**

The exercises which follow are designed to help you identify your personal values, and begin the process of aligning what you do with those values. This is about you as an individual. Your values are personal to you; they stay the same wherever you are, although you may or may not feel able to express them in particular situations.

The exercises won't identify your personal values for you! They are designed to give you an opportunity and a framework in which to think about what your personal values might be, and decide for yourself. There are no 'good' values or 'bad' values; no 'right' values to choose and no 'wrong' values. 'Honesty' is not better than 'Happiness'!

Throughout these exercises, the list of possible values is not 'complete'. They are examples, and include most of the values that we have seen people identify over a period of years. If you want to choose values that are not on the list, feel free to do so; write them into the spaces at the end of the list.

### 1. Identify Your Personal Values

Go through the list of values which follows, and score each one out of ten by ringing the appropriate number. The more important that value is to you, the higher the score; the less important it is, the lower the score.

In scoring the values, you may find it helpful to think about such questions as:

- Which values are the most important to me?
- Which values really represent who I am?
- What values do I most want to demonstrate in my life?
- What words would I most want to hear others using to describe me?
- Which of these characteristics do I most admire in others?

Similarly, if you find a certain kind of behaviour particularly annoying that may be an indicator that its opposite is one of your key values. For example, if secrecy makes you particularly angry, that suggests that Honesty is important to you; if you cannot stand people being treated unfairly, perhaps Fairness or Justice should receive a high score.

When you've finished scoring all the values on the list, write the highest scoring values in the spaces on the right of the page, up to a maximum of six. You may find that your scores suggest a smaller number. For example, if your top scores are 10, 9, 9, 8, 6, 6, 5 … you may feel that the first four values are the ones that really matter. In our experience, you should settle on no less than three. But remember, this is not a numbers-based exercise. Listen to your heart, not your head!

| VALUES | | | | | | | | | | |
|---|---|---|---|---|---|---|---|---|---|---|
| Accountability | 1 | 2 | 3 | 4 | 5 | 6 | 7 | 8 | 9 | 10 |
| Authenticity | 1 | 2 | 3 | 4 | 5 | 6 | 7 | 8 | 9 | 10 |
| Commitment | 1 | 2 | 3 | 4 | 5 | 6 | 7 | 8 | 9 | 10 |
| Compassion | 1 | 2 | 3 | 4 | 5 | 6 | 7 | 8 | 9 | 10 |
| Contribution | 1 | 2 | 3 | 4 | 5 | 6 | 7 | 8 | 9 | 10 |
| Creativity | 1 | 2 | 3 | 4 | 5 | 6 | 7 | 8 | 9 | 10 |
| Determination | 1 | 2 | 3 | 4 | 5 | 6 | 7 | 8 | 9 | 10 |
| Enthusiasm | 1 | 2 | 3 | 4 | 5 | 6 | 7 | 8 | 9 | 10 |
| Excellence | 1 | 2 | 3 | 4 | 5 | 6 | 7 | 8 | 9 | 10 |
| Fairness | 1 | 2 | 3 | 4 | 5 | 6 | 7 | 8 | 9 | 10 |
| Freedom | 1 | 2 | 3 | 4 | 5 | 6 | 7 | 8 | 9 | 10 |
| Fulfillment | 1 | 2 | 3 | 4 | 5 | 6 | 7 | 8 | 9 | 10 |
| Generosity | 1 | 2 | 3 | 4 | 5 | 6 | 7 | 8 | 9 | 10 |
| Happiness | 1 | 2 | 3 | 4 | 5 | 6 | 7 | 8 | 9 | 10 |
| Honesty | 1 | 2 | 3 | 4 | 5 | 6 | 7 | 8 | 9 | 10 |
| Integrity | 1 | 2 | 3 | 4 | 5 | 6 | 7 | 8 | 9 | 10 |
| Justice | 1 | 2 | 3 | 4 | 5 | 6 | 7 | 8 | 9 | 10 |
| Leadership | 1 | 2 | 3 | 4 | 5 | 6 | 7 | 8 | 9 | 10 |
| Learning | 1 | 2 | 3 | 4 | 5 | 6 | 7 | 8 | 9 | 10 |
| Loyalty | 1 | 2 | 3 | 4 | 5 | 6 | 7 | 8 | 9 | 10 |
| Openness | 1 | 2 | 3 | 4 | 5 | 6 | 7 | 8 | 9 | 10 |
| Partnership | 1 | 2 | 3 | 4 | 5 | 6 | 7 | 8 | 9 | 10 |
| Passion | 1 | 2 | 3 | 4 | 5 | 6 | 7 | 8 | 9 | 10 |
| Respect | 1 | 2 | 3 | 4 | 5 | 6 | 7 | 8 | 9 | 10 |
| Responsibility | 1 | 2 | 3 | 4 | 5 | 6 | 7 | 8 | 9 | 10 |
| Self-expression | 1 | 2 | 3 | 4 | 5 | 6 | 7 | 8 | 9 | 10 |
| Trust | 1 | 2 | 3 | 4 | 5 | 6 | 7 | 8 | 9 | 10 |
| Vision | 1 | 2 | 3 | 4 | 5 | 6 | 7 | 8 | 9 | 10 |
| Wisdom | 1 | 2 | 3 | 4 | 5 | 6 | 7 | 8 | 9 | 10 |
|  | 1 | 2 | 3 | 4 | 5 | 6 | 7 | 8 | 9 | 10 |
|  | 1 | 2 | 3 | 4 | 5 | 6 | 7 | 8 | 9 | 10 |
|  | 1 | 2 | 3 | 4 | 5 | 6 | 7 | 8 | 9 | 10 |
|  | 1 | 2 | 3 | 4 | 5 | 6 | 7 | 8 | 9 | 10 |
|  | 1 | 2 | 3 | 4 | 5 | 6 | 7 | 8 | 9 | 10 |
|  | 1 | 2 | 3 | 4 | 5 | 6 | 7 | 8 | 9 | 10 |

*The Real Game's Personal Values Workbook.* © the real game 2005    www.therealgame.biz

My highest scoring values are:

_____

_____

_____

_____

_____

_____

## 2. Review:

Review your list of up to six personal values. Are you comfortable that you've got the right list? As we said at the beginning, the exercises are designed to help you identify your personal values. They won't identify your values for you! So make any changes to the list that you wish. Just because 'Passion' scored less than 'Creativity' doesn't mean that you can't choose Creativity and leave Passion out. The intention is that you arrive at a list that you feel genuinely represents your personal values.

On the other hand, it doesn't have to be perfect! Your choice is not irreversible! If, as time goes on, you change your mind about one or more of the values – change them!

- _____
- _____
- _____
- _____
- _____
- _____

## 3. Define:

Write short descriptions of what each of those values mean to you. That isn't necessarily a definition, and you certainly won't find it in the dictionary (although you may want to see what the dictionary says). What does that value mean? What does/could it provide in your life? What does it require of you? How will you behave?

Again, this is another opportunity to review your choice of values. You may find that as you try to write your description of one of the values, you realise that actually it doesn't really matter to you. Or you may find that what you write is actually a description of another value altogether. If so, change it!

There is no 'right' format. It may be one or two elegant sentences; five or six short phrases; or a combination. A good approach is to brainstorm words and phrases that you associate with that value, and then work out how to fit some or all of them together afterwards (see the format which follows).

We'd suggest 20-40 words for the final definitions, but don't be constrained by that recommendation. If you feel the need to write half a page about each value, go ahead. What matters is that the finished thing accurately captures what the value means for you, and that it accurately reflects an aspect of who you are.

## Defining Personal Values

**Value:**

**Brainstorm:**

**Definition:**

## 4. ACTIONS

Those values are only meaningful to the extent that you actually align your behaviour with them; and the process of aligning your behaviour with your personal values is a life's work!

It starts with identifying simple actions that you should start or stop. In this context, 'actions' are specific things that you are going to do or stop doing, that are an expression of each of your personal values.

Some may be 'one-off' actions; things you do once that are then complete. For example,

- apologise to X
- get a new job
- climb a mountain
- marry my boy/girlfriend

Others will be ongoing;

- go to the gym three times each week
- work one day per month for a charity
- save 15% of my personal income
- attend quarterly community association meetings

Some you could relate to either way; is "stop smoking" a one-off or ongoing? That's your decision.

We recommend six 'start' actions and six 'stop' actions, with a balance between oneoff and ongoing. 'One-off' actions are great for generating momentum; ongoing actions are, well, ongoing….

One clear 'don't'; avoid statements on principle. It may be true that your value requires you to 'tell the truth', 'listen to people', or 'stop stealing' (!). However, statements of principle are notoriously hard to put into action. In any case, they will either be explicitly included in your values definitions, or self-evident to you.

Review and update your actions regularly. When a one-off action is complete, replace it with another (climb next mountain; apologise to Y; organise second honeymoon…). When an ongoing action loses its sparkle, update it. "go to the gym three times a week" might become "go to the gym or go running three times each week'.

*The Real Game's Personal Values Workbook.* © the real game 2005    www.therealgame.biz.

PERSONAL VALUES

| Value: |  |
|---|---|
| **Definition:** | |

<table>
<tr><td colspan="2" align="center">**Actions**</td></tr>
<tr><td>**Start**</td><td>**Stop**</td></tr>
<tr><td>1</td><td>1</td></tr>
<tr><td>2</td><td>2</td></tr>
<tr><td>3</td><td>3</td></tr>
<tr><td>4</td><td>4</td></tr>
<tr><td>5</td><td>5</td></tr>
<tr><td>6</td><td>6</td></tr>
</table>

## 5. Making This Work

Finally, a statement of the glaringly obvious; these exercises will not produce the results for you! Ultimately, it's a matter of your personal discipline.

With that in mind, we finish with two recommendations:

- Schedule a two hour 'values review' for yourself every month for the next twelve months. Do it when it works for you; the first Saturday morning of the month, the last Friday evening before you leave work, or whatever is practical for you. But put it in the diary now.
- Ask someone to act as your coach. Share the materials with them; and ask them to manage you on your actions. Make promises about when things will be done, and ask them to follow up.